FROZEN IN TIME

FROZEN IN TIME

The Greatest Moments at the Winter Olympics

BY BUD GREENSPAN

Foreword by Juan Antonio Samaranch
Preface by Bonnie Blair

GPG
GENERAL
PUBLISHING
GROUP, INC.

Publisher: W. Quay Hays
Editorial Director: Peter L. Hoffman
Editors: Amy Spitalnick, Dana Stibor
Art Director: Robert Avellan
Production Director: Trudihope Schlomowitz
Prepress Manager: Bill Castillo
Production Artist: Gaston Moraga
Production Assistants: Tom Archibeque, David Chadderdon, Gus Dawson, Russel Lockwood, Regina Troyer
Copyeditors: Mark Lamana, Karre Marino

Back cover photo: UPI/Corbis Bettmann

For information:

General Publishing Group, Inc.
2701 Ocean Park Boulevard, Suite 140
Santa Monica, CA 90405

Library of Congress Cataloging-in-Publication Data

Greenspan, Bud.
    Frozen in time : the greatest moments at the Winter Olympics / by
Bud Greenspan.
        p. cm.
    ISBN 1-57544-027-X
    1. Winter Olympics—History.   I. Title
GV841.5.G74   1997
796.98—dc21   97-29735
                                                CIP

Printed in the USA
by RR Donnelly and Sons Company, Inc.
10 9 8 7 6 5 4 3 2 1

General Publishing Group
Los Angeles

TABLE OF CONTENTS

Foreword 11

Preface 13

Introduction 15

Sonja Henie 19

Eric Heiden 21

Franz Klammer 25

Eugenio Monti 27

Better Late Than Never: Anders Haugen 31

Raisa Smetanina 35

Oksana Baiul 37

Andrea Mead Lawrence 41

Colin Coates 43

Veikko Hakulinen and Sixten Jernberg 47

Lydia Skoblikova 51

The Great Controversy: Jean-Claude Killy and Karl Schranz 53

Three Friends from Hokkaido: Japan's Ski Jumpers of 1972 57

Dick Button 59

Tenley Albright 63

Dietmar Schauerhammer and Wolfgang Hoppe 65

The First Great Hockey Upset 69

Karin Kania 71

Alberto Tomba 75

Gunde Svan 79

The Russian Invasion: Pairs Figure Skating 83

Bill Koch 87

Irving Jaffe 89

Rosi Mittermaier 93

Birger Ruud 95

Torvill and Dean 99

Toni Sailer 101

The 1960 United States Hockey Team: The Team of Destiny 105

Christa Rothenburger 107

Vegard Ulvang and Bjørn Dælhie 111

Billy Fiske 115

Gillis Grafström 117

The Goitschel Sisters 121

Magnar Solberg 123

Johann Olav Koss 127

Matti Nykänen 129

The Jenkins Brothers 133

Carol Heiss 135

Leonhard Stock 139

Maurilio De Zolt 143

Gaetan Boucher 145

Bonnie Blair 149

Peggy Fleming 151

Phil and Steve Mahre 155

Myriam Bédard 157

Yvonne van Gennip 161

Ulrich Wehling 163

Jack Shea 167

Manuela Di Centa and Lyubov Egorova 169

Bill Johnson 173

Dorothy Hamill 175

Tomas Gustafson 179

Brian Boitano and Brian Orser 181

The Miracle on Ice 185

Katerina Witt and Debi Thomas 187

Dan Jansen 191

Winter Olympic Sites 195

Records of the Winter Olympic Games 196

Photo Credits 208

To Nancy Beffa, who, as always, makes it all happen.

SPECIAL THANKS

To Eric Hamilton, Suzanne Beffa, and Sydney Thayer, who gave up their evenings and weekends and were in fact, for a year, *Frozen In Time*.

To Bill Mallon, author of *The Golden Book of the Olympic Games*, for his advice.

FOREWORD

BY JUAN ANTONIO SAMARANCH
PRESIDENT, INTERNATIONAL
OLYMPIC COMMITTEE

Following the success of his *100 Greatest Moments in Olympic History*, Bud Greenspan, member of the Olympic Order and for four decades the premier producer, writer, and director of Olympic films, now gives us *Frozen In Time: The Greatest Moments at the Winter Olympics*.

This most recent publication, which heralds the opening of the XVIII Olympic Winter Games in Nagano in February 1998, pays tribute to the greatest sportsmen and -women who have taken part in Olympic Winter competition. Once again, Bud Greenspan presents a comprehensive look at this very special class of athletes, whose embodiment of the ideals and values of the Olympic movement is captured in powerful images and thoughtful words.

Competition in the Olympic Winter Games requires athletes to overcome special challenges, and the joy of their victories is all the more radiant. With his 40 years of experience chronicling the history of the Olympic movement and spreading the spirit of friendship and peace to which we all aspire, Bud Greenspan shares in this book his intimate understanding of our movement, which he has honed throughout this career.

On the event of the Olympic Winter Games, which will draw this millennium to a close and chart our course for the next, it is fitting that the Olympic family should pay tribute to one of its dearest friends.

On behalf of the Olympic movement, therefore, I should like once again to express my heartfelt congratulations to Bud Greenspan for this new publication and for his lifelong commitment to the promotion of the Olympic spirit.

Juan Antonio Samaranch
Marqués de Samaranch

PREFACE

By Bonnie Blair

As a four-time Winter Olympian, I am excited about the publication of *Frozen In Time* by Bud Greenspan. As the ultimate authority on the Olympic Games, he is better suited than anyone to document this history. Every Olympiad has its own special stories that should be told. Of the four Olympics in which I competed, each one has its own special place in my heart.

Although I did not medal in Sarajevo in 1984, I will never forget my time there. I was then an unknown participant in awe of being surrounded by so many athletes I admired. I could not believe that I could sit in the athletes' cafeteria with heroes such as Scott Hamilton and Phil Mahre. And the people of Sarajevo were wonderfully gracious. In no other Olympics have I seen people's homes and hearts so open to competitors from around the world. It is painful to see what has happened to these extraordinary people in the years since.

I especially enjoyed the Olympics because I was not just competing for the speed skating team but also for the entire U.S. team, comprising competitors in a variety of sports. One of my greatest honors was being selected to carry the American flag during the Closing Ceremonies of the Winter Olympics in Calgary. It was very touching to be chosen not just by my colleagues in speed skating but by the entire U.S. team for this honor. Hearing our national anthem played as a result of my achievements brought tears to my eyes and inspired me to continue competing, even though most people had a hard time understanding why I did not quit once I had a gold medal. Competing in a sport you love adds much more to your life than just medals. You will understand this better as you read Bud's book.

I remember Albertville mainly from the additional pressure I experienced as a returning gold medalist. This felt very different from being an excited young skater who was just happy to be in the Olympics. I came with expectations by the media to prove myself, and I was very proud that I did so and was even able to walk away with two additional gold medals.

Lillehammer will always remain very special in my heart not only because I was able to win two gold medals and end my Olympic career on a high note but also because of the perfect setting Lillehammer provided for the Olympic Games. It was very cold and snowy, truly a "winter wonderland." The people of Norway were incredible in that they rooted for every athlete, no matter what country he or she hailed from. Athletes felt as if they had the whole world cheering them on.

Attending my first Summer Games (as a spectator, of course) in Atlanta in 1996 helped me to appreciate the Winter Games even more. The Summer Games are overwhelming in their range. With fewer sports and fewer countries competing, the Winter Games are much more intimate. You feel like you get to know the athletes from other countries much better.

In the midst of Olympic competition—made more special by being held only every four years—an individual can truly understand the feeling of world peace for the 16 days the Games take place. There are also so many inspirational stories of athletes who have overcome incredible hardship to reach the Olympic Games, whether they win a medal or not. It is through these stories, so perfectly told by Bud Greenspan, that the reader can be motivated to achieve—whatever his or her chosen field.

INTRODUCTION

BY BUD GREENSPAN

History records the first Winter Olympic Games as being held in 1924, in Chamonix, France, but several winter sports were contested as part of earlier Olympic Games.

Figure skating events were held at the 1908 London Olympics, but four years later, Sweden refused to schedule any winter events at their 1912 Stockholm summer program. World War I canceled the 1916 Summer Olympics, and when the Games were renewed in the summer of 1920 in Antwerp, figure skating and ice hockey events were added to the regular program.

Four years later, the Winter Games became official in Chamonix, and they were an instant success—highlighted in retrospect by the appearance of an 11-year-old Norwegian figure skater named Sonja Henie.

Similar to the Summer Games, the Opening Ceremonies of the Winter Games are a celebration. Hundreds of athletes march into the stadium in a prelude to the competitions that are to come. For the athletes, to enter the Olympic stadium is in itself the fulfillment of a lifetime of training, even though only a few will actually stand on the awards podium.

So what is it that inspires these athletes to give so much of their lives in the attempt? Surely it is the belief in their individual talent; surely it is pride; surely it is courage. But it is more than these. Perhaps, most of all, it is a dream—a dream that one day, for a few moments at a given time and place, something magical will happen: a performance that will earn them the right to stand on one of three steps of the awards podium and for all time be known as a medal winner at the Olympic Games.

There is an old maxim that "valor consists of doing without witnesses that which we would be capable of doing before an audience." The Winter Olympian embodies this belief perhaps more than any other athlete. Downhill skiers test their courage hundreds of times in preparation for just one 80-mile-per-hour trip down the course at the Olympic Games. Day in and day out, bobsledders challenge injury and physical handicap in their quest to traverse the course a hundredth of a second faster than on their previous run. Ski jumpers seek out space and distance, preparing for the day when the gold medal will be contested.

As in all things, there is always one performance that, though many times equaled or surpassed, defines a momentous achievement and forever inspires those who follow. Hundreds have run the mile in less than four minutes, but Roger Bannister of Great Britain was the first. The scaling of Mount Everest will forever be associated with Sir Edmund Hillary, and those who followed are all but nameless. Neil Armstrong was the first man to walk on the moon, joined by others whom few can remember.

The Winter Olympic Games have seen their share of those incredible performances—some remembered, others almost totally ignored. To this day, Sonja Henie is the only female skater to win three successive individual gold medals. But what about the men? Almost totally unknown and unheralded is figure skater Gillis Grafström of Sweden, who won three successive gold medals eight years before her (1920–1928).

Who can forget the incomparable performance of America's Eric Heiden at the 1980 Lake Placid Games, winning all five men's speed skating events? Yet almost totally unknown is Lydia Skoblikova of the Soviet Union, who won all four women's speed skating races in four consecutive days at the 1964 Innsbruck Games—in addition to the two gold medals she'd won four years earlier, giving her the all-time record of six.

Then there is the performance of Jean-Claude Killy of France, who became world-famous after winning all three alpine skiing events at the 1968 Grenoble Games. But who remembers the name Toni Sailer, of Austria, the first man to accomplish that feat 12 years earlier at the 1956 Innsbruck Games?

"True endurance is to endure the unendurable," a Japanese philosopher once wrote. Many an athlete has used these words to overcome seemingly insurmountable handicaps and obstacles in the quest for Olympic glory. But win or lose, the honor is in the attempt—the benchmark for all those who enter the arena in the never-ending pursuit of excellence.

"The honor should not go alone to those who have not fallen—rather all honor to those who fall and rise again," is an expression that can be associated with many athletes who have endured a lifetime quest for Olympic greatness. They are the persistent ones who taste defeat, then come back in a continual reach for the stars, and finally succeed.

While there are many reasons an Olympian returns to the arena, often the words of President Theodore Roosevelt, written almost a century ago, inspire them: "It is not the critic who counts. The credit belongs to the one who is actually in the arena, whose face is marred by dust, sweat, and blood, who errs and comes up short again and again, and who, at the worst, in failure, at least fails while daring greatly—and whose place shall never be with those cold and timid souls who know neither victory nor defeat."

This book is the story of those who have made the attempt—the men and women of the Winter Olympics whose efforts fulfill the words that have lived through the ages: "Ask not alone for victory. Ask for courage, for if you can endure, you bring honor to yourself. Even more, you bring honor to us all."

SONJA HENIE

History has been unkind to Herma Planck-Szabó of Austria, who won the 1924 women's figure skating gold medal in Chamonix, France, the scene of the first Winter Olympic Games. Instead, the women's championships are best remembered for the appearance of an 11-year-old girl from Norway, who finished in last place. Her name is Sonja Henie, and today, more than seven decades later, she is still the most famous figure skater ever to have stepped onto the ice.

Sonja Henie was a creation of her father, Wilhelm, a former world-class cyclist. He realized that Sonja not only had great talent as a skater but also had a personality that captivated audiences both on and off the ice. He decided to capitalize on her physical charm, dressing her for competitions in outfits more suited to an actress than a figure skater.

When she was 15, she gained worldwide fame at the St. Moritz Olympic Games. Six of seven judges gave her performance top honors, winning Henie her first gold medal. It was the American judge who gave her a second place vote behind Beatrix Loughran, one of two U.S. women in the competition. It was not considered coincidental that the Norwegian judge gave Loughran a seventh place vote.

For the next eight years, Sonja Henie ranked with the superstars of the day in other sports: Bill Tilden in tennis, Babe Ruth in baseball, Paavo Nurmi in running, and Jack Dempsey in boxing. Her fame had spread to the United States even though few Americans had ever seen her compete.

At the 1932 Olympic Games in Lake Placid, Henie received first place votes from all seven judges. Soon, offers for personal appearances came from U.S. promoters, as well as from around the world.

Leading to the 1936 Olympic Games in Garmisch-Partenkirchen, Henie let it be known that this would be her last Olympics, and that she would retire after the world championships one week later. She wanted to go out with a flourish— three Olympic gold medals and 10 straight world championships—for that was a Hollywood ending, and starring in motion pictures was next on her agenda.

Ironically, the woman who gave Henie her greatest challenge at the 1936 Games was Britain's Cecilia Colledge, a 15-year-old. Colledge's career closely followed Henie's. Four years earlier, when Henie won her second gold medal, 11-year-old Colledge finished eighth—the same position at the same age as Henie in her first Olympics at Chamonix.

At age 23, Henie was now the "old lady" of the figure skating competition, and Colledge was the teenager on the rise. Skating before Chancellor Adolf Hitler and his entourage, Henie prevailed. As the last of 26 skaters, she received six first place votes and shared a seventh with Colledge.

Her Olympic dreams fulfilled, Sonja left Europe to pursue her dreams of Hollywood fame and fortune. She was an immediate success, and before her motion picture career was over, she had starred in 10 films. She became a U.S. citizen in 1941, and for many years was criticized for not doing enough for her native Norway, which was occupied by the Germans for more than five years during World War II.

Nevertheless, when, after the war, she returned to Norway for skating exhibitions, the response to Henie was the same as it had been before—she played to sold-out, loving audiences.

Henie was married three times, the last time to her childhood sweetheart, millionaire shipbuilder Niels Onstad. But the rumor persisted throughout her film career that her true love was actor Tyrone Power, her costar in her second Hollywood film.

Sonja Henie was the most successful of any athlete in her transition to the movie screen. Beyond her marriages to millionaires, she herself was worth nearly $50 million when she died of leukemia in 1969 at the age of 57. Her memory lives on in Oslo, where she and her third husband established the Henie-Onstad Museum and Cultural Center, which houses an outstanding collection of modern art.

ERIC HEIDEN

In early February 1979, a year before the 1980 Lake Placid Games, 20-year-old Eric Heiden of the United States won all four men's events at the world championships in Oslo: the 500, 1500, 5000, and 10,000 meters. His victories confirmed his legendary status in Norway, a country that treats its own superstar speed skaters with reverence.

His acclaim throughout Norway and Europe was comparable to that of a rock star, as Heiden was besieged by the public to the point that police escorts were needed wherever he went. His esteem was such that "The Ballad of Eric Heiden" was one of Norway's most popular songs.

Heiden's rise to the top was a surprise to many, for as a 17-year-old at the 1976 Innsbruck Olympics, he finished seventh in the 1500 meters and 19th in the 5000 meters, his only two races. But in the years between Innsbruck and Lake Placid, he developed into an icon, capable of winning races at every distance—500 meters to 10,000 meters. His prowess as an all-arounder brought unabashed praise from Norwegian coach Sten Stenson.

"In Norway, we say that if you can be good in the 5000 and 10,000 meters," said Stenson, "you cannot be world-class in the 500 meters. Eric is the only one who can do it. We have no idea how to train our skaters to compete against him. It's like having the best sprinter in the world entering the marathon and winning it. We just hope he retires soon."

At the 1980 Lake Placid Games, the 21-year-old Heiden entered all five men's events, and the predictions were almost unanimous that he would win at least two and medal in all five.

Up to that point, there had been only one clean sweep of gold medals in speed skating: At the 1964 Innsbruck Olympics, Lydia Skoblikova of the Soviet Union won all four women's events—to go along with the two gold medals she'd won four years earlier in Squaw Valley.

Heiden's first event was the 500 meters—the lone race in which most experts considered him vulnerable. Additional pressure was placed on Heiden when he drew the first pair with world record holder Yevgeny Kulikov of the Soviet Union. Most skaters prefer skating in later pairs so they know what times they have to beat. Nevertheless, skating against the world record holder to start off the competition didn't faze Heiden.

"I have always skated because it's fun," Heiden said before the race. "I've seen

how it is with foreign skaters—the pressure from sponsors, coaches, the public, and even from government. American skaters are loose compared to them. We're out to have a good time."

Heiden's coach, Dianne Holum, herself a gold medal winner at the 1972 Sapporo Games, greatly admired his ability to relax.

"It takes years of concentration to learn to relax while competing," said Holum. "Some skaters never learn. Eric was special. He learned early."

In the 500 meters, Heiden trailed Kulikov by $5/100$ of a second after the first 100 meters. This was worrisome for Heiden supporters. The whole race takes less than 40 seconds, leaving little time to make up any deficits.

"The 500 goes so quickly," said Heiden. "You have time to correct mistakes in the longer races, but not in the 500 meters."

Inch by inch, Heiden made up the distance and on the last turn, skating the inside lane, catapulted into the lead. At the finish, he was $34/100$ of a second ahead of Kulikov, and with that, he set an Olympic record. Kulikov ended up with the silver medal.

The following day in the 5000 meters, Heiden was nearly five seconds behind the leader with one-third of the race over. Without panicking, the 6-foot 1-inch 185-pounder went into full throttle and won the race by a little less than a second, again setting an Olympic record.

In his third race, the 1000 meters, he again turned in an amazing performance, winning by a second and a half.

Two days later, he tied Lydia Skoblikova's record of four gold medals, winning the 1500 meters by more than a second.

On Saturday, February 23, the last day of the speed skating competition, Heiden would make his historic attempt in the 10,000 meters. The night before, he had cheered himself hoarse as one of the spectators at the American hockey team's amazing upset of the Soviet Union.

The 10,000 was supposed to be Heiden's toughest race, for in it he would compete against long-distance specialists who were well rested for this event. It turned out to be a glorious climax to the most spectacular performance by an individual in speed skating history.

Heiden not only won by an unthinkable 7.9 seconds, but he also broke the world record by six seconds.

Afterward, he was asked to describe his greatest moment of the Games.

"That's simple," said Heiden, as modest as ever. "It was last night, when I saw the United States beat the Russians in the hockey game. God, that was great."

Franz KLAMMER

Sixty-thousand spectators surrounded the downhill run at the 1976 Innsbruck Games. From their incredible roar, one might assume they were all Austrians. For at the top of the hill, the 15th starter was their national hero, 22-year-old Franz Klammer. Even before the Games got under way he had become a living legend.

Most alpine skiers would be content to win any Olympic medal. Franz Klammer did not have that choice. Nothing but victory would satisfy his countrymen. The entire nation would go into mourning if all Klammer could garner was a silver or bronze.

Yet Klammer himself was responsible for the high expectations of his fans.

The year before the Games, Klammer had won eight straight downhill races, and leading to Innsbruck he'd won another four. But those victories would have no meaning if the Austrian national anthem was not played in his honor at the Games when his country was host nation.

The Olympic course at Patscherkofel was a demanding one: almost two miles of curves and bumps with the skier traveling at 70 miles an hour. But its perils were not unknown to Klammer. One year earlier, he won a downhill race on the same course.

By the luck of the draw, Klammer would start in the 15th position, which gave him an advantage. The best skiers would have already finished their runs, so Klammer would know the time he would have to beat. He also was still glowing from the response he received from thousands of his countrymen the day before, when he carried the Austrian flag into the stadium during the Opening Ceremonies.

Despite all the publicity he'd received, he was not the only favorite for the gold medal.

"I was most concerned about the two Swiss," recalled Klammer. "Bernhard Russi won the downhill four years before in Sapporo and was the defending champion, and his teammate, Philippe Roux, was capable on any given day of turning in a winning performance."

As Klammer waited for his start time at the top of the hill, his predictions about the Swiss seemed justified. Russi was in the lead, followed by Herbert Plank of Italy. Roux was in third place. Only 63/100 of a second separated first and third.

Klammer could hear the roar of "Franzi...Franzi...Franzi" rising from the thousands of Austrians watching from below as he waited for the countdown.

Klammer dashed out of the starting gate as if he had been shot from a cannon. It soon became evident that he would go for broke—be either a strong contender for the gold medal or one of the skiers who came crashing down the slopes, the victim of the treacherous, icy course.

"You have only one chance in the downhill," said Klammer. "Unlike the slalom races where you have two runs, there is no chance for error. You go all out and pray for the best."

Halfway down the course, Klammer was almost a fifth of a second behind Russi.

Arms flailing, Klammer was a spectacular—if not a pretty—picture. Several times it appeared he would, like several before him, become a victim of the course.

Coming into the last 1000 meters, Klammer was flying. He almost missed a gate, but he seemed to sense that now the outcome of the race was in his hands.

At the bottom, Bernhard Russi waited. Although Klammer was only the 15th of more than 70 contestants, Russi knew the gold and silver medals would be decided in the last few seconds of Klammer's run.

As Klammer neared the finish, the cries of "Franzi...Franzi...Franzi" grew louder. The spectators at the bottom switched their focus back and forth from the speeding dot in the yellow uniform to the scoreboard ticking off the seconds.

When Klammer crossed the finish line, Russi knew the result without looking at the scoreboard. The roar from the crowd told him. Klammer had defeated him by $^{33}/_{100}$ of a second in a race that many still consider the greatest in downhill history. With this single victory, Klammer became the most acclaimed skier in Austrian Olympic history—even more renowned than Toni Sailer, who had won all three alpine events 20 years earlier.

One bit of irony followed: Four years later, Franz Klammer was not considered good enough to make the Austrian downhill team that competed in Lake Placid. However, he came back in 1984, finishing 10th in the downhill at the Sarajevo Games.

EUGENIO MONTI

For a man who gets seasick on a cruise ship and woozy in a jetliner, it's a wonder Italy's Eugenio Monti came to be considered by many the greatest bobsled driver in history.

"I don't mind ships or airplanes," said Monti. "It's my stomach that doesn't like them."

The word *fear* is not in Eugenio Monti's vocabulary. Before he became a bobsledder, he was considered one of the best downhill skiers in the world after he won the 1951 Italian Championship. But preparing for the 1952 Oslo Olympics, he severely injured his knees in a terrible accident, and his competitive career appeared to be over.

Two years after his accident, Monti and a few friends decided to enter an amateur bobsled race. None had ever been on a sled before, and not one would volunteer to be the driver. Instead they all pointed toward Monti. The result was his first victory—one of many that would take place over the next 16 years.

He was considered a sure thing in both the two- and four-man events at the 1956 Games, held in his hometown of Cortina d'Ampezzo. He knew the course perfectly, but all he could garner was two silver medals.

"I was terrible in Cortina," said Monti. "I knew the course better than anybody. But my sled was no good...but that was not the main reason I lost. It was just that I was no good."

The 1960 site in Squaw Valley, California, had no bobsled course, so 32-year-old Monti attended the Games as a spectator but vowed that he would compete in the 1964 Innsbruck Games.

There, Monti gained additional fame but not because he won. He came in third in both the two- and four-man events but gained glory as the ultimate sportsman for loaning a bolt to the British team when one of theirs broke. The British sled, driven by Tony Nash, went on to win the two-man gold medal.

"They told me it was a very gracious act," said Monti, "but Tony Nash was a very good driver that day, and he deserved to win."

Although he was widely acclaimed for his sportsmanship, Monti was depressed.

"I was 36," said Monti. "I was getting old, and I believed that it was not my fate to win a gold medal."

Monti then went into retirement.

Two years later, Monti's brakeman in the two-man event, Sergio Siorpaes, designed a new and faster sled.

When Monti took it on a practice run, his enthusiasm of the past returned, and they won the two-man event at the 1966 World Championships.

The following year, the world championships were held at the new track near Grenoble, France, as a test for the Olympic Games one year later.

Again, misfortune struck Monti and, in particular, his brakeman, Sergio Siorpaes.

Monti and Siorpaes were well in the lead coming into the final turn on their final run. But then tragedy struck. The rough and spotty course had been a problem throughout, and the imperfections finally caught up with them.

At the peak of the turn, the sled flipped. Monti and Siorpaes were thrown, and the sled landed on top of them.

Miraculously, Monti emerged with only minor scratches, but Siorpaes' arm was broken so severely that he would be unavailable for the Grenoble Olympics.

Monti had long ago lost count of his serious accidents, but sitting beside his partner's hospital bed, he wondered if this was a sign he should finally retire. With nine world championships, he was already the winningest bobsledder of all time.

Even so, Monti chose the relatively inexperienced Luciano De Paolis as his new brakeman, and continued pursuit of the one honor that had eluded him for 12 years.

At age 40, he would make his final attempt.

At the Grenoble Olympics, the two-man event was scheduled to be contested over two days—two runs each day.

Because of the warm weather, the course had become rough and choppy. Officials decided to start the event at 5:00 A.M. to take advantage of the cold morning air before the sun rose.

After the first two runs, Monti and De Paolis led the second place West German team by $24/100$ of a second.

But in their first run the following day, they lost the lead by $1/10$ of a second to the Germans.

"I was terrible. It was all my fault," said Monti. "I was starting to believe again that I would never win the gold medal. I was not confident at all."

But Monti was wrong. On his fourth and last run, he was superb. He tore down the course and the team's time of 1:10.05 was the fastest of the competition and a new course record.

"After finishing my last run, I decided to join my friends in the Italian radio booth and watch the Germans go down," said Monti. "I was very nervous."

The Germans started off magnificently. Halfway down the course, they were faster than Monti's new record. But as they neared the finish, they ran into trouble on two steep turns, losing valuable fractions of a second. As they crossed the line, their time was flashed on the scoreboard.

"They were a tenth of a second behind my last run, but their four-run total was exactly the same as ours," said Monti. "We were told that we each would earn the gold medal."

But then the officials went to the rule book.

"Then we learned that one of the rules stated that if there was an overall tie," said Monti, "the victory would go to the team with the fastest individual run. Our record fourth run was the fastest, so the gold medal was ours."

A few days later, Monti drove his four-man team to another victory. One month after his 40th birthday, Eugenio Monti had fulfilled his lifelong dream—to become an Olympic champion—twice.

BETTER LATE THAN NEVER

The first Winter Olympic Games took place in Chamonix, France, in 1924, but it took 50 years for the final result in the first Olympic ski jumping contest to become official.

As expected, athletes from Norway and Finland dominated the Games, winning 27 of the 43 medals awarded.

There were two individual stars of the Chamonix Games. In speed skating, Clas Thunberg of Finland dominated his opponents. In five events, he won three gold medals, a silver, and a bronze.

The other great superstar was 29-year-old Thorleif Haug of Norway, who led his countrymen to a near sweep of the cross-country and ski jumping events.

On January 30, 1924, the grueling 50-kilometer cross-country event was contested. When it was all over, Haug had won the gold medal, followed by two fellow Norwegians, who had won the silver and bronze.

Three days later, Haug again was spectacular, winning the 18-kilometer cross-country race by more than a minute over his teammate Johan Gröttumsbråten. Tapani Niku of Finland broke the string of Norwegian medalists by winning the bronze.

On February 4, the final day of the Games, the ski jump was scheduled. Again, a sweep was predicted for the Norwegians, with Haug having the opportunity to win two more medals at one time—one for the ski jump and one for the nordic combined event, which would add the results of the ski jump and the 18-kilometer race that Haug had already won.

Although Haug's two leaps were barely good enough to win him a bronze medal in the ski jump, they easily earned him the gold in the nordic combined. That night, Haug would return to Norway a national hero, with three gold medals and one bronze. So enamored were the Norwegians of Haug's performance that he would be given another honor: His hometown of Drammen erected a statue of him while he was still alive.

But while the Norwegians were celebrating Haug's magnificent performance, a contingent of Americans at the ski jump in Chamonix watched in disbelief. They were certain that 35-year-old Anders Haugen, the Norwegian-born American champion, had actually beaten Haug in the ski jump event and should have been awarded at least the bronze medal.

At 36, Anders Haugen was the captain of the first U.S. Olympic nordic ski team in 1924.

Haugen, who had paid his own way to Chamonix, turned in two spectacular leaps. Using a new style—leaning forward over the tips of his skis—he tied for first place in the first round, then came back with the longest leap of the day in the second round.

Though Haugen had the longest combined distance, when the official results were posted, he was placed fourth behind Haug and two other Norwegians. The Americans watching the event were astounded and threatened an official protest. Since the ski jumping contest is decided by distance and style, the judges claimed that Haugen's unorthodox style was inferior to the three Norwegians placed above him, thus it was proper to place him fourth. Haugen returned to the United States and continued to win competitions until he finally retired in obscurity—though his aerodynamic jumping style became the standard in ski jumping for decades to come.

In February 1974, a half-century after the 1924 Chamonix Games, the surviving Norwegian athletes held a 50-year reunion. One of the athletes, Thoralf Strömstad—who had finished second behind Haug in the nordic combined—brought a 1924 official results book to the reunion. There, he and historian Jakob Vaage found an error that had gone unnoticed for 50 years.

In the battle for the bronze medal in ski jumping, Thorleif Haug had been awarded 18.000 points to Anders Haugen's 17.916. But incredibly, the judges had added Haug's score incorrectly. He had actually scored 17.821. What the American fans had suspected 50 years earlier had at last been discovered to be true. Anders Haugen had actually won the bronze medal that day.

The climax of the story was one of the most dramatic moments in all of sports history. On September 12, 1974, a special ceremony was held at the Holmenkollen in Oslo, the most legendary ski jump site in all of winter sport.

There, as the Norwegian heroes of 1924 watched, a wrong was righted. There were tears in the eyes of many spectators as 85-year-old Anders Haugen was presented with the bronze medal by Thorleif Haug's daughter, who had kept her father's medals after his death 40 years earlier.

With this ceremony, history was made. Anders Haugen remains the only American ever to have won an Olympic ski jumping medal.

RAISA SMETANINA

There is a saying that has sent Winter Olympic athletes into the arena since the start of the Winter Games in Chamonix, France, in 1924: "Ask not alone for victory, ask for courage. For if you can endure, you bring honor to yourself. Even more, you bring honor to us all."

No athlete better exemplifies these words than the Soviet Union's Raisa Smetanina, one of the legends of cross-country skiing.

Smetanina was 23 years old when she competed at the Innsbruck Games in 1976. In her first event, the 5 kilometers, she won the silver medal, finishing just a little more than a second behind Helena Takalo of Finland. No one suspected that it was the beginning of the career of a living legend.

The following day, Smetanina got sweet revenge in the 10 kilometers. In one of the closest races in Olympic history, she defeated Takalo by $87/100$ of a second.

Two days later, Smetanina skied the third leg for the Soviet 4 x 5-kilometer relay team. Again she was superb, setting the stage for teammate Galina Kulakova, skiing the anchor leg, to finish well ahead of Takalo and give the Soviets the gold medal.

Four years later in Lake Placid, Smetanina continued her winning ways. She captured the gold in the 5 kilometers and anchored the Soviet relay team that won the silver medal. In two Olympics, she had won three gold and two silver medals.

Smetanina was approaching 32 when the 1984 Sarajevo Olympics got under way. She continued her medal-winning performances by taking two more silvers—in the 10 kilometers and the 20 kilometers.

"People ask me why I continue to compete," said Smetanina. "Why not? I'll continue to ski as long as I can win medals."

Smetanina was 35 years old when she made the team that would compete at the 1988 Calgary Games. There, she won the silver medal in the 10 kilometers and the bronze in the 20 kilometers. She now had won nine medals in four Olympics, tying for top honors with Sixten Jernberg of Sweden, winner of four gold, three silver, and two bronze medals in cross-country skiing at the 1956, 1960, and 1964 Games.

"The older you get, the harder it gets," Smetanina said. "But when you accomplish what you set out to do, it is worth all the work...all the pain."

Four years later, Smetanina was named to the Unified Team that would compete in the 1992 Albertville Olympics. The Unified Team was made up of athletes who had competed for the Soviet Union before its breakup. In the 15 kilometers, Smetanina finished fourth behind rising star Lyubov Egorova.

Smetanina was also selected to ski the second leg in the 4 x 5-kilometer relay. In a thrilling duel with Norway, which was highlighted by a magnificent last leg by Egorova, the Unified Team won by more than 20 seconds.

After winning her 10th medal in her fifth Olympics just days before her 40th birthday, Smetanina was asked if she would finally retire and make room for younger athletes. "Younger athletes?" she replied. "Hey, I'm really only 10 years old. Why should I retire now?" Smetanina was a leap-year baby, born on February 29, 1952.

But the 1992 relay would be Raisa Smetanina's last Olympic race. Her gold medal entered her in the record book as the greatest medal winner in Winter Olympic history, with a total of 10—four gold medals, five silver, and one bronze. In addition, she is the only athlete to win medals in five different Winter Olympic Games. But perhaps the best testimony to her legacy can be found in the words of her teammate, Lyubov Egorova, who in Albertville was the star of the Games, taking three gold and two silver medals:

"When I was a little girl, my idol was Raisa Smetanina. My ambition was one day just to meet her. You can imagine what it meant to me in Albertville when we were on the same team and able to join together to win the relay. Of all my victories, I will remember that the most, for she was my inspiration."

OKSANA BAIUL

The women's figure skating competition at the 1994 Lillehammer Games was filled with drama long before the skaters stepped onto the ice.

For weeks preceding the Lillehammer Olympics, the sports world had been mesmerized by daily reports implicating America's Tonya Harding in a vicious attack against teammate Nancy Kerrigan shortly before the Olympic trials.

Kerrigan recovered from her knee injury and was given special dispensation to join the American team even though she did not compete in the Olympic trials. Through a series of legal maneuvers, Harding was also permitted to skate in the Olympics.

Figure skating is a two-discipline event: The competitors skate a required technical program on the first night, followed two evenings later by a four-minute free-skating event.

At the end of the technical program, Kerrigan was in first place, followed by 16-year-old Oksana Baiul of Ukraine. Harding was out of medal consideration, finishing in 10th place after the technicals.

But at a practice session the day before the free-skating final, Baiul collided with another skater, suffering severe injuries to her right leg and back. For Baiul, it was just another roadblock to overcome in a career that was star-crossed.

Baiul's life had been filled with tragedy. She never knew her father, who left home when she was a small child. Her grandparents, with whom she lived, both died when she was growing up. Her mother died of cancer when Oksana was 13.

When Baiul was 14, her skating coach, Stanislav Korytek, moved to Canada from Ukraine, and he hoped to take his protégé with him. But once in Canada, Korytek realized the difficulty that would be involved. He suggested that Baiul work under the tutelage of Galina Zmievskaya, the famed coach of the 1992 men's Olympic champion, Victor Petrenko, who was married to Zmievskaya's daughter.

"When Stanislav Korytek suggested that I coach Oksana, I was not excited at first," Zmievskaya said. "I don't like to work with someone else's students. I like to prepare them from the beginning—it's like a housewife cooking borsch without outside help. Besides, she had no place to stay, and I had just a small home with two children. But Victor Petrenko, who had been helping her for years, said to me, 'She is such a small girl...how much can she cost? How much can she eat?'" The decision was made—Baiul would be added to her new coach's family.

Nancy Kerrigan of the United Sates, Oksana Baiul of Ukraine, and Chen Lu of China.

"Galina and Victor mean everything to me," Baiul said. "They not only coach me, they are my family. I do not know why I have been so fortunate to have those two. Nobody else in the world would do for me what they have done."

Baiul has been compared to the legendary Sonja Henie, the only skater in history to win three Olympic gold medals. Henie won her first gold medal when she was 15, Baiul's age when she catapulted to the world stage with a spectacular victory at the 1993 World Championships.

Nancy Kerrigan failed to medal in that competition, but as the skaters prepared for the free-skating program in Lillehammer, Kerrigan was in the lead, with the injured Baiul in striking distance.

Twenty-four women would skate that night, divided into four sections of six skaters. Kerrigan and Baiul would skate in the final six.

Kerrigan went on before Bauil and was spectacular. Many Americans believed it to be a gold-medal performance. All nine judges gave her first place marks both for technical merit and artistic impression. But there was still room for Baiul to challenge her for the gold medal.

"I remember my name being announced," Baiul said, "and I waited for my music to start. I had to wait and concentrate because there were children on the ice collecting all the flowers for Nancy Kerrigan, so I had to wait before I could begin my program."

In the stands, Galina Zmievskaya was also waiting for the music to start.

"For anybody else, this delay would have been a disaster," Zmievskaya said. "But Oksana is so determined and of such a strong will, I knew it would not affect her."

Both Zmievskaya and Baiul knew that the first jump was the most critical part of the program, for earlier, with the approval of the International Olympic Committee, Baiul had received painkilling injections for her injuries from the preceding day.

Baiul performed her first jump, a triple lutz, perfectly, the first of five triples on her program. The rest of her program was nearly perfect, but the final decision was still in doubt.

Soon the final tabulation was announced, and it was almost impossible to believe. Of the nine judges, four gave first place votes to Baiul, and four placed Kerrigan in the top spot.

The ninth judge called it a tie, but according to the rules, ties are broken by the skater with the highest artistic score. The judge had given Kerrigan a 5.8, while his score for Baiul was 5.9. By $1/10$ of a point, Oksana Baiul was the Olympic champion.

ANDREA MEAD LAWRENCE

Twenty-eight-year-old Gretchen Fraser and 15-year-old Andrea Mead were the old and young women of the American women's slalom team competing at the 1948 St. Moritz Games.

For Fraser, it was the end of an eight-year wait. She had made the 1940 Olympic team, but the Games had been canceled that year and in 1944 because of World War II.

Andrea Mead had surprised the skiing world by winning the slalom at the 1948 U.S. Olympic Trials, defeating Fraser by almost five seconds.

But in St. Moritz, Fraser showed her greatness. She won the event, with Mead finishing eighth.

Gretchen Fraser became the first American, male or female, to stand on the top of the awards podium for alpine skiing—a position that in the past had been the exclusive domain of European skiers.

When Fraser retired after the St. Moritz Games, Mead took over. At the age of 18, Mead married David Lawrence, a member of the U.S. men's ski team.

As the 1952 Oslo Games approached, Andrea Mead Lawrence was practically unbeatable. There was speculation that she could medal in all three events on the women's program.

In her first event, the giant slalom, she confirmed the predictions of those who believed her to be the world's best alpine skier. In an event usually decided by hundredths of a second, Andrea won by more than two seconds.

"I've always said that you can't win unless you're having fun," she said afterward. "I've been skiing since I was three years old, not to win but to have fun. And it's always been that way with me—having fun."

Three days later, Andrea was going after her second gold medal, competing in the downhill. From the start, it appeared that she was on the way to her second victory. But then, disaster struck. She fell.

"There is such a thing I call extension, or the 'perfect line,' in skiing," she said. "I overextended when I fell. Interestingly, I was so far ahead at that point that I still could have won. I got up but fell a second time, and that was it."

The slalom was scheduled for three days later—two runs down a gated course, with the lowest combined time determining the winner. Andrea was the fifth skier out for the first run. Again, in the upper part of the hill, she was the fastest of all. But again, she lost her perfect line, and her ski caught a gate. Balancing herself a few meters past the gate she had missed, she came to a complete halt, then quickly backtracked to get back on the course. Then, as if starting the race over from the standing position, she finished her run. Incredibly, she was in fourth place, 1.2 seconds behind the leader.

"As I got ready for the second run, an amazing thing happened," she recalled. "I was actually smiling looking down the course. But I didn't see ice or the gates. I was seeing an image of this enormously deep, black, still pool. And there was total silence. And then I heard the countdown: 5-4-3-2-1. I must have been smiling down the entire second run."

Her second run was spectacular, flawless.

"I waited at the bottom of the hill for the others to go down," she said. "But I was confident. I had skied the perfect line."

When the final skier completed the course, Andrea Mead Lawrence had made Olympic history. She was in first place, almost a second faster than the second place finisher, becoming the first female alpine skier to win two gold medals in the same Olympic Games. To this day, she is the only American to have won two alpine gold medals.

Between Oslo and the 1956 Cortina Olympics, Andrea gave birth to three children but amazingly continued to win races. She again made the U.S. Olympic team in 1956 and, at age 23, finished fourth in the giant slalom, missing the bronze medal by $^1/_{10}$ of a second.

Although she retired from Olympic competition after the 1956 Games, Andrea Mead Lawrence received one more Olympic tribute—the honor of being the final torchbearer for the Opening Ceremonies of the 1960 Squaw Valley Games.

COLIN COATES

Australia is one of four countries that have competed in every Summer Olympic Games since the modern revival in Athens in 1896. When one thinks of Australian athletes, the immediate image that comes to mind is water—Australia being the home of great swimmers and rowers. But one of the most dramatic stories of Australian Olympic history occurred in a most unlikely place—the speed skating competitions at the Winter Olympic Games.

While Colin Coates may not be a household name, his persistence and talent have placed his name in the record book. He is the only athlete to compete in six successive Olympic speed skating competitions—a 20-year span from 1968 through 1988.

Coates, a plumber by trade, was an exceptional athlete. He was a three-time Australian speed skating champion, a triple Australian champion in the 14-foot sailing dinghy, an excellent hockey player, and a cyclist who, many believe, had championship potential. Once, a horrendous skiing accident left him with two broken arms and a smashed nose and jaw. Although he had 10 metal pins inserted into his body, three weeks later, he was back at the rink entering speed skating competitions.

Coates began his Olympic career at age 21 as one of the three Australian athletes to compete at the 1968 Grenoble Olympic Games. He entered two events, finishing 41st in the 500 meters and 49th in the 1500 meters. Since there was no speed skating oval in all of Australia, between Olympics, Coates would live and train in Holland, where he continued to work as a plumber.

"He could have won some Olympic medals if he were born Dutch or Scandinavian," said one Australian Olympic official. "Those countries revere speed skating, and they could have molded him into a champion."

Coates competed in all four events at the 1972 Sapporo Olympics, where his highest finish was 18th in the 10,000 meters. His participation, however, went all but unnoticed, for the star of the Games was Holland's Ard Schenk, who won three gold medals—in the 1500, 5000, and 10,000 meters.

Five skiers and 29-year-old speed skater Colin Coates were the six Australian athletes marching in the Opening Ceremonies of the 1976 Innsbruck Games.

Coates entered all five speed skating events. On February 14, 1976, he made Australian Olympic history, finishing in sixth place in the 10,000 meters. Although

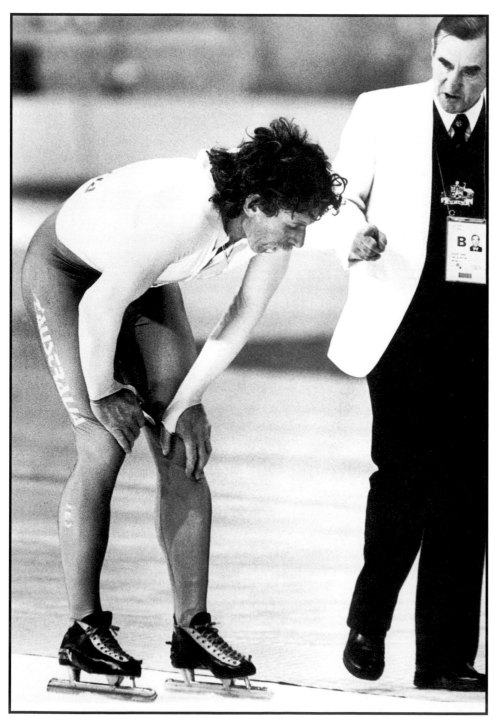

At the end of the 10,000 meters, Australian team manager Geoff Henke finally caught up with Colin Coates.

he was more than 25 seconds slower than the winner, his sixth place was the highest finish of any Australian athlete in any Winter Olympic sport.

At the 1980 Lake Placid Games, 33-year-old Coates entered three events—the 1000, 5000, and 10,000 meters, finishing well back in all three races. His fourth straight Olympic appearance was overshadowed by Eric Heiden, who himself made Olympic history by winning all five races on the men's program.

Four years later, at the Sarajevo Games, Coates' highest finish was 22nd in the 10,000 meters. Incredibly, though he was 37 years old, he was skating faster than ever.

As the 1988 Calgary Games approached, Coates wanted to make one more attempt. In five previous Olympics he had stepped to the starting line 17 times without ever coming close to winning a medal. Yet, with this losing but admirable record, he will most fondly be remembered for his final Olympic appearance at age 41 at the 1988 Calgary Olympic Games.

Although Coates was already coaching, he asked to skate as a member of the Australian team. His federation turned down his request. After much heated discussion with Australian officials, Coates was named coach-manager of the speed skating team. They agreed to put his name on the team as a potential participant but only so that Coates could mingle on the ice to train and share his experiences with the younger team members.

"Colin knew that his name was placed on the 'competitor' list purely for technical reasons," said Geoff Henke, the manager of the 12-man Australian team in Calgary. "Colin understood this and agreed to it, and I trusted that he would live up to the agreement."

Historically, Australian athletes have been known for their *joie de vivre*. Throughout the years, nodding "yes" has often meant "maybe." Coates was no exception.

A few days before the 10,000 meters was scheduled, Danny Kah, a young Australian who was entered in the event, scratched, leaving an open spot. Coates just couldn't resist and entered his own name in the draw. He drew the last pair of the night, usually considered the best starting spot—but not for Coates.

"I was hoping to draw the first pair, so I could get out there, skate my race, and clear out before anyone noticed," he explained. "As it was, my name would be up there all night like a sitting duck."

Coates was so paranoid about being discovered that he didn't even sleep in the village that night. He stayed at a friend's house in Calgary so that people would think he was out on the town all night and wouldn't suspect that he was racing the next day.

The night of the race, two athletes accompanied Coates to the rink to give him split times. He stayed hidden in the locker room, waiting until the last minute to take the ice. Then he took a quick warm-up and went to the starting line.

"I was in the team quarters at the village when the 10,000 meters was being run," said Henke. There was a crowd of athletes in front of the television, blocking Henke's view. "I looked in and couldn't believe it. I thought it was a replay of past Olympics. But there was Colin Coates, in the official Australian uniform, at the starting line. I rushed out to the arena, my main purpose being to drag him off the ice. When I arrived there, he was halfway through the race, so I decided to let him finish."

Coates was having the race of his life. The public address announcer had reported that Coates was making Olympic history—tying the record for most

appearances—and the stadium was going wild. With the crowd behind his every stride, Coates set a new Australian record.

Soon after he crossed the finish line, Coates was on the receiving end of a tongue-lashing from Henke, for reasons unknown to the thousands in the stands. Soon Henke realized he'd better not make a major issue of it—all of Australia was paying tribute to Coates, who would receive hundreds of congratulatory telegrams.

"I guess I shouldn't have done it," Coates said afterward. "But when I received a telegram from Prime Minister Bob Hawke saying all of Australia was proud of me, maybe it was the right thing to do after all." At age 41, after six successive Olympics, Colin Coates said farewell to the arena. He left as he'd intended—skating the fastest 10,000 meters of his career.

VEIKKO HAKULINEN AND SIXTEN JERNBERG

The vast snow-covered lands of Scandinavia are steeped in mystical traditions that are centuries old, harking back to ancient times when hunters traveled great distances on skis.

It follows, then, that when cross-country skiing became part of the Olympic Games, athletes from Scandinavia and Finland would dominate the sport. In the first six Winter Olympics, beginning in Chamonix in 1924, every cross-country medal was won by a skier from Finland, Sweden, or Norway. This is understandable, for children in Europe's northland often learn to ski before they can walk.

From 1952 to 1964, two men dominated the sport: Veikko Hakulinen of Finland and Sixten Jernberg of Sweden. History records those years as the Hakulinen-Jernberg Era.

"I am four years older than Sixten Jernberg," Hakulinen recalled. "He did not compete at the 1952 Oslo Games, when I was fortunate enough to win the 50-kilometer race. But we raced many times leading to the 1956 Olympics in Cortina, and the world waited to see who would be victorious."

In Cortina they would both compete in all four races: the 15 kilometers, 30 kilometers, 50 kilometers, and 4 x 10-kilometer team relay.

"Veikko Hakulinen and I had two of our best races at the 1956 Cortina Olympics," recalled Jernberg. "My starting time was before Hakulinen's in the 30-kilometer race, so when I finished, he was still on the course. Waiting at the finish line, I looked at the clock as Veikko approached the finish, and I knew I would have to settle for the silver medal. He defeated me by 24 seconds."

Jernberg got his revenge in the grueling 50-kilometer race. He defeated Hakulinen, the defending champion, by more than a minute. When the competition was over, little separated the two rivals: Hakulinen had captured a gold and two silver medals, while Jernberg had earned a gold, two silver, and a bronze.

Four years later, the rivalry continued at the 1960 Squaw Valley Games. There, the 35-year-old Hakulinen would win a gold, a silver, and a bronze, while Jernberg would finish with a gold and a silver.

Hakulinen retired after the 1960 Games, but Jernberg went on to win two more gold medals and a bronze at the 1964 Innsbruck Olympics, earning

Veikko Hakulinen after winning his third and final gold medal, Squaw Valley, 1960.

him one of the greatest Olympic records in history—four gold, three silver, and two bronze medals.

"We were rivals in the competition," Hakulinen recalled. "But we were good friends. Win or lose, we would sit down afterward and discuss the race. I have been in many competitions, but there was something very special when Sixten was in the race."

"The press would always emphasize the rivalry between Veikko and me," said Jernberg. "But rivalries produce lifetime friendships. Veikko was a true sportsman, and I cherish those days when we competed against each other."

Although they both competed in three Olympics, the Hakulinen-Jernberg Era was named specifically for their meetings in 1956 and 1960. In those head-to-head contests, each man won two gold medals, three silver, and one bronze. And perhaps that is the way it should be, for both were legends in their time, born to the snow-covered lands where cross-country skiing had its beginnings many centuries ago.

Sixten Jernberg at Cortina, 1956.

Lydia Skoblikova setting an Olympic record in the 1500 meters in Innsbruck—her second gold medal in two days.

LYDIA SKOBLIKOVA

Women's Olympic speed skating was introduced at the 1960 Squaw Valley Games with four events on the program. At Squaw Valley, too, began the Olympic career of Lydia Skoblikova of the Soviet Union, whom many still consider the greatest woman speed skater in history.

In Squaw Valley, Skoblikova, a 20-year-old school teacher, entered three events. She won both the 1500- and 3000-meter races but finished fourth in the 1000 meters, more than a second behind the winner, teammate Klara Guseva.

Two years later at the world championships, Skoblikova was outclassed by teammate Inga Voronina, who over a two-day period created world records in the 500, 1500, and 3000 meters.

Not to be outdone, Skoblikova made speed skating history the following year by sweeping all four events—the 500, 1000, 1500, and 3000 meters—at the 1963 World Championships in Japan.

The skating world now looked forward to the 1964 Olympic Games in Innsbruck and the battle between Skoblikova and Voronina. But it was not to be. Still weak from a severe stomach ailment, Voronina was unable to make the 1964 Soviet Olympic team.

In Innsbruck, Skoblikova, now 24, entered all four events. It was expected that she would at least repeat her double–gold medal performance of four years earlier in Squaw Valley.

Her first race was the 500 meters, the distance at which she was most vulnerable.

Skating in the first pair, her teammate Irina Egorova, the Soviet Union's top sprinter, set the standard for the day with a time of 45.4.

Egorova's time held up through the next 13 pairs. The next-to-last pair included Lydia Skoblikova. As she approached the finish line, Skoblikova was relentless. She beat Egorova's time by 40/100 of a second, setting an Olympic record.

"I was worried most about the 500 meters," Skoblikova recalled. "One mistake can cause you to lose the race. I knew I had to skate a perfect race to beat Egorova."

The next day, the 1500 meters was scheduled. Skoblikova was again superb. She defeated second place finisher Kaija Mustonen of Finland by almost three seconds to break her own Olympic record.

The following day she would again have to face Egorova in the 1000 meters.

"After my victories in the 500 and 1500 meters, I had great confidence," said Skoblikova. "The 1000 was one of my favorite distances, and I held the world record."

The 1000 meters is 2 1/2 laps around the 400-meter track. Again, Skoblikova skated flawlessly, defeating Egorova by more than a second to set her third Olympic record of the Games.

"I am happy but tired," Skoblikova said that night. "I have raced three races in three days. Now, I must concentrate fully on the 3000."

The following day, the thousands in the stands could sense that they were about to witness Olympic history. For the fourth successive day, Lydia Skoblikova would step to the starting line—this time to place her name in the record book as one of the immortals.

As she circled the track, the crowd cheered her every stride. When she crossed the finish line, the crowd gave her a thunderous ovation. When the last of the skaters finished, Skoblikova was the winner by more than 3 1/2 seconds.

Four years later, at the 1968 Grenoble Games, 29-year-old Lydia Skoblikova returned to the ice to compete in the 1500 and 3000 meters. But she was not the Skoblikova of old. She failed to place in either of the events.

Today, Skoblikova still graces the Winter Olympic record book. With six gold medals, she is tied with her countrywoman cross-country skier Lyubov Egorova for the most gold medals in a career. That record may someday be broken. But Lydia Skoblikova's performance at the 1964 Innsbruck Games—winning all four speed skating gold medals on four successive days—will live for all time.

THE GREAT CONTROVERSY

On February 17, 1968, the men's slalom was scheduled at the Grenoble Winter Olympic Games. For France's magnificent Jean-Claude Killy, it figured to be a historic day—his opportunity to win the third and final jewel of the alpine skiing crown.

Eight days earlier, Killy had come hurtling down the course in the downhill to defeat countryman Guy Perillat by 8/100 of a second and win his first gold medal.

Four days afterward, on February 12, Killy won the giant slalom by an incredible 2.22 seconds for his second gold medal. Almost four seconds behind him in sixth place was his archrival, Karl Schranz of Austria. No one knew at the time that the two would soon become embroiled in the most controversial race in Winter Olympic history.

As the slalom was about to get under way, anticipation was high that Killy would win the triple—all three alpine events—to join Austria's Toni Sailer, who had accomplished that feat 12 years earlier, at the Cortina Olympics.

Fifty-six men had qualified for the slalom final, to be run over a twisting, tightly gated course at Chamrousse, near Grenoble.

But when the skiers arrived at the top, a dense fog choked the mountain. All week, the fog had wreaked havoc with the racing, but now it seemed impenetrable. The racers looking down the course could see no farther than two gates in front of them.

"If you leaned over a little and adjusted your binoculars," one columnist wrote, "you probably could see your feet."

Television executives from many countries, particularly the United States, pleaded for a postponement, since some 300 million people around the world would see no more than gray ghosts occasionally appearing on their screens.

The protests were made to no avail. The French authorities defiantly announced, "The race must go on."

On the first run, Killy started in 15th position, and when the round was completed, he was in first place. Schranz also had a good run and was a close third, just hundredths of a second behind Killy.

In spite of hopes that the fog would clear, between rounds the weather worsened.

Killy was the first man down the course for the second run. When he crossed the finish line, the thousands of French spectators cheered wildly—not only because his time was commendable, but because he was able to find the finish line.

Killy's gold medal in the 1968 downhill was his first in his attempt to win skiing's triple crown.

The celebration continued as skier after skier missed gates or fell, but soon depression spread among the French as it was learned that one of the ghosts whom nobody could really see, Häkon Mjön of Norway, had taken first place away from Killy.

Though he apparently was in first place, Mjön was unsure if he had skied all the gates. When asked, he just shrugged his shoulders. Soon, the French were cheering again. It was announced that Mjön had missed a couple of gates on his way down and was disqualified. Killy was still in first place but was very worried about Schranz, who was about to start his run.

"We were at the bottom of the hill, waiting for Schranz to finish," Killy said afterward, "but he never arrived."

Up in the fog, Schranz had aborted his run at the 22nd gate, one-third of the way down the course.

"I saw this shadow walking across the course," Schranz explained. "There was no way I could continue."

The Austrians quickly protested, claiming a course policeman had walked onto the course just above the gate. Their cause was supported by two officials and another skier.

Schranz was granted a rerun, and his performance was spectacular; he finished with a combined time 24/100 of a second faster than Killy's. For the second time, Killy had apparently been shoved out of first place; Schranz was declared the unofficial winner. But would Killy have to settle for the silver medal?

The controversy raged throughout the afternoon, with the French protesting that Schranz had missed two gates just before aborting at the 22nd gate of his original run. In effect, they contended that Schranz should have been disqualified during that run and the rerun should never have taken place.

Schranz was uncertain, saying, "If I missed a gate, I did not realize it. I was hypnotized by the dark shadow I saw ahead of me. It is possible I missed a gate to avoid the shadow."

Finally, a five-hour jury meeting was held. By a vote of 3–2, Schranz was disqualified for missing the gates on his first run. Jean-Claude Killy, the greatest Alpine skier ever, had won his third gold medal.

Yukio Kasaya making history on his second jump at the 1972 Sapporo Games.

THREE FRIENDS FROM HOKKAIDO

On February 3, 1972, 1,128 athletes representing 35 countries marched in the Opening Ceremonies of the Sapporo Winter Olympic Games. It was the first time an Asian city would host the Winter Games, though not the first time Japan would be honored with hosting the Olympics.

Eight years earlier, Tokyo had greeted the summer athletes. Although the Tokyo Games were hailed throughout the world as a brilliant success, privately the Japanese people felt there was one embarrassing failure: They were unable to win a gold medal in track and field, the marquee event of the Games.

Many in Japan feared further embarrassment at the 1972 Sapporo Games, for Japan's Winter Olympic history was all but devoid of success. Leading to the 1972 Games, Japan had won only a single medal—a silver in the slalom by Chiharu Igaya at the 1956 Cortina Games.

So at 10:00 A.M. on Sunday, February 6, 1972, millions of viewers throughout Japan nervously stared at their TV sets awaiting the start of the 70-meter ski jump.

At the bottom of the hill, more than 100,000 spectators, mostly Japanese, were waiting to cheer Sapporo's hometown hero, 28-year-old Yukio Kasaya, to victory. Leading to the Sapporo Games, Kasaya had won three straight championships on the European circuit, becoming Japan's best hope for a gold medal.

There was additional excitement for the Japanese spectators, for joining Kasaya on the ski jumping team were two other local ski jumpers from the island of Hokkaido, where Sapporo is situated. They were 27-year-old Akitsugu Konno and 29-year-old Seiji Aochi. All three were born during World War II.

Fifty-six jumpers were entered in the competition. The crowd would have to wait for its hero, as Yukio Kasaya would be the 45th contestant to jump.

But they did not have to wait long to explode with tumultuous cheering, for the fifth jumper was Akitsugu Konno, who immediately leaped into first place with a jump of 82.5 meters.

His lead held until the 20th contestant—teammate Seiji Aochi.

Aochi's leap was one meter longer than Konno's, and his style points were superior. Aochi went into the lead, followed by Konno in second place. Incredibly, Japanese jumpers already held the top two spots, and their number-one champion Kasaya had yet to jump.

Twenty-four skiers followed Aochi; not one of them could supplant the two Japanese. Finally, it was time for the 45th jumper, Yukio Kasaya.

The thousands at the bottom of the hill, including Japan's Emperor Hirohito, fell silent as Kasaya paused at the start. Then, as he sped down the ramp, a roar arose from the crowd, leading into a crescendo as he lifted off. By the time he landed, the noise was deafening. Kasaya had leaped 84 meters, the longest jump of the first round. When he received 57 out of a possible 60 style points, he moved into the lead by more than three points. With one round to go, the Japanese held all three medal positions.

In the second round, Konno and Aochi traded places in the standings when Konno surpassed Aochi in both distance and style points. Konno took over the lead, with Aochi right behind him.

This was but a prelude of what was to come, for everyone was waiting for Kasaya's second attempt.

Finally, Kasaya stepped to the platform. For him, this was the moment of truth. High above the silent crowd, he appeared to be a statue, staring down the run without moving a muscle. Then, slowly, he bowed his head. Looking up again, he gazed down the runway, then lowered his head once more. The wait seemed interminable.

At last Kasaya started down, the crowd roaring as he lifted off. He soared majestically through the air, and when he landed perfectly, the crowd knew the result before it was posted. He had tied his teammate Akitsugu Konno for the longest second jump. But with nearly impeccable style points, the gold medal was his.

The celebration at the bottom of the hill was glorious. Kasaya's Japanese coaches, defying a stoic tradition, wept openly. Kasaya was greeted by his brother Akio and his teammate Konno. As the three embraced, the crowd gave a standing ovation.

History was made that day in Sapporo. With all of their nation watching, Japanese athletes, who had won but a single medal in previous Winter Olympics, had swept all three medals in the 70-meter ski jump.

DICK BUTTON

After a 12-year hiatus caused by World War II, the Winter Olympics were resurrected in St. Moritz in 1948. In four prior Olympic Winter Games, no American male figure skater had been able to win an individual gold, silver, or bronze medal. But this unenviable record was expected to end, for one of the favorites for championship honors was 18-year-old Dick Button, a Harvard freshman from Englewood, New Jersey.

"When I was 12 years old," Button recalled, "I went to a skating rink in New Jersey for some lessons. The teacher said I never would learn how to skate 'until all hell froze over.' I guess, physically, she was right. I was a short kid, about 5 feet 2 inches, and I weighed 165 pounds. She didn't say it, but I'm sure she was thinking, 'Why would I want to be seen with that funny little fat boy?' Fortunately, my father overheard her and announced, 'If my son wants to be a skater, he can be a skater, and I'll get him the best lessons and the best of everything.'"

Button certainly made use of "the best of everything." He came to dominate the sport and in St. Moritz received eight of the nine first place votes for an easy victory. Additionally, he received a perfect score of 6 from several of the judges—the first time a figure skater had been so honored.

"I think it was an explosion of athleticism that I brought to the sport...bigger moves...bigger jumps," Button said. "There were a number of things I introduced that male skaters had never done before...not only in jumping but in spinning. I was the first to do a camel spin. Men never considered it as part of their repertoire." When Button returned home following the Games, he was invited to the White House by President Truman.

Four years later, 22-year-old Dick Button was the heavy favorite to defend his championship. He came to the 1952 Oslo Games with four successive world championship wins to his credit. Despite such impeccable credentials, when he got ready to perform, he was as nervous as a novice.

"It's the most excruciating, horrendous, petrifying feeling. It's just a horrible moment. I remember feeling like a knife was turning in my stomach," Button said. "I remember walking around in circles and muttering to myself, 'I don't need this. I don't have to do this. Why don't I just quit and lead a normal life!'"

For Button, winning the gold medal was not enough. There was an additional challenge, a personal one: He was there not only to defeat his opponents. He was there to challenge himself.

"One of the reasons for putting yourself on the line," Button said, "is that life is not simply treading water...I always felt that once you reach a certain point, you have to try and move ahead."

Button lived his philosophy to the hilt at the Oslo Games. To his technically challenging program, he added the triple loop—a move that had never before been accomplished.

"I could have played it safe and won the competition without trying the triple loop," Button said. "But the win would not have satisfied me without making the attempt. If I didn't try it, I would have gone through my entire life with an emptiness."

In his free-skating routine, Button mesmerized the crowd and the judges as he had done four years before, particularly after performing the triple loop. When he came to a twirling finish, bravos filled the arena and smiles lit up the faces of all nine judges as they marked their scores, unanimously placing Button as the Olympic champion. Yet, even with this magnificent performance behind him and his Olympic career at a triumphant end, a sense of fulfillment eluded him.

"I was satisfied with my performance," Button said, "but it was not my best. I think I reached my peak a few days before the competition began. I really think I was only 99 percent the day I won."

After his retirement, Button became a television producer, and he has long been regarded as the preeminent television commentator on figure skating. Even more, Dick Button will be most remembered as the skater who revolutionized the sport—the winner of seven national championships, five world championships, and two Olympic gold medals.

TENLEY ALBRIGHT

On July 18, 1935, at his New Jersey home, future figure skating legend Dick Button was celebrating his sixth birthday. That same day, a baby girl named Tenley Albright was born in Newton, Massachusetts. Besides a lifetime of celebrating their birthdays on the same day, they would also share a page in figure skating history, for they were the first American male and female skaters to win Olympic gold medals.

"Dick showed us all how boundless the possibilities were in skating," Albright said. "He had such a powerful presence that we could always tell the moment Dick had entered the rink, even during our practice. There would be a respectful silence, with great anticipation. We knew that as soon as he stepped onto the ice, he would do something new, something far beyond our dreams."

At the 1952 Oslo Olympics, the 22-year-old Button thrilled the skating world by winning his second successive gold medal, repeating his triumph in St. Moritz.

The day before, all eyes had been on the women's competition, where 16-year-old Tenley Albright stood a good chance of becoming America's first female skater to stand on the top step of the awards podium.

Albright's appearance in Oslo was in itself phenomenal. Five years earlier, when she was 11 and skating for just two years, she contracted polio. It was feared that she would never skate again.

"Fortunately, I was not completely paralyzed," Albright said, "but for a time it was quite scary. I didn't have full use of my leg, neck, and back. Eventually, the doctors allowed me to go back to skating as part of my therapy."

Albright completely recovered, so much so that she began competing and winning championships. When she was 16, she was nominated to go to the 1952 Oslo Olympics and won the first of five successive national championships.

In Oslo, she finished second behind Jeannette Altwegg of Great Britain. Altwegg had built a large lead in the compulsories and was able to hold off Albright's superb effort in the free-skating program. Ironically, the British judge gave Albright his first place vote, but six of the nine judges placed the British champion first.

By today's rules, Albright would probably have won, since the compulsories, which in 1952 comprised 60 percent of the total score, have been eliminated from the competition.

The year following the Oslo Games, Albright became the first American woman to win the world championship title. She came in second the following year, and then regained her title in 1955. Most experts predicted she would become an Olympic champion the following year in Cortina. To prepare for that challenge, Albright took a semester off from her pre-med studies at Radcliffe College. She arrived in Cortina a few weeks before the Games were to begin and practiced twice a day.

"One day, we were practicing outdoors," Albright recalled. "It was a beautiful sunny day, and we were all laughing and joking and going through our routines. Without warning, my skate hit a rut in the ice. I can usually brace myself for a fall but couldn't this time. The blade of my skate slashed through my right boot. The cut went right to the bone. It was a jagged cut, very messy, but fortunately it didn't break any bone.

"I called home to my father, who was a surgeon, and he flew to Cortina and fixed me up. But I couldn't do any serious jumps or spins. Then, I remember quite clearly that on the morning the competition was to begin, I tried out my routines. Thank goodness, it felt just as it did before the injury."

Albright held a slight lead over her young teammate, Carol Heiss, in the compulsories and was in a commanding position to win it all.

"I remember the music starting," she recalled. "I had chosen to skate to 'The Bacarolle' from *The Tales of Hoffman*. Then suddenly I heard singing. I knew my music was just orchestral, but now I heard singing...like a chorus. What happened was the thousands watching were humming and singing along with the music. It was wonderful. It made me forget about my injury."

Albright completed her program to a resounding roar from the spectators. The crowd had declared her the winner—but they had no official votes.

"It's wonderful how we get results today with computers," Albright said with a smile. "But in Cortina, we had to wait for what seemed hours and hours. We would try to add up the scores and see if we could figure out the results. We'd make mistakes in addition and then tally them over and over again. It was nerve-racking."

Finally, the judges' decision was announced. Albright had worried for no reason. Ten of the 11 judges gave her first place votes. The lone dissenter was the American judge, who gave his vote to Heiss.

Albright became the first American woman to win an Olympic gold medal. But that night at the awards ceremony, she was part of another first.

"The victory ceremony was beautiful," Albright said. "The lights from houses on the surrounding mountains were like stars. I waited expectantly to sing along to 'The Star Spangled Banner.' But then, 'My Country 'Tis of Thee' started to play. It was just beautiful."

There is one lasting ritual that binds Tenley Albright and Dick Button. Every year on July 18, one calls the other to share a happy birthday wish.

DIETMAR SCHAUERHAMMER
AND WOLFGANG HOPPE

Dietmar Schauerhammer of East Germany had hopes of making the 1980 Summer Olympic team in the decathlon. But severe injuries prevented him from competing in the 1980 Moscow Games.

"I was very disappointed," Schauerhammer said. "It was particularly difficult because I knew the injuries would prevent me from ever competing on a world-class level. The year after the Moscow Olympics, my good friend Wolfgang Hoppe, also a decathlete, suggested we try a new sport as a team. It turned out to be a very good suggestion."

Bobsledding became their sport, with Hoppe the driver and Schauerhammer the brakeman. Soon they became the most feared team in the sport.

At the 1984 Sarajevo Winter Games, after Hoppe and Schauerhammer won the two-man gold medal, they were joined by two teammates to capture the gold in the four-man event. They then looked forward to repeating their victories at the 1988 Calgary Games. But as the Games approached, an injury to Hoppe started a chain reaction that would cause an injury to Schauerhammer.

"Because of his injury, Wolfgang was not able to run at the start," Schauerhammer recalled. "That is the most critical part of the race. So we practiced starts with Wolfgang already in the sled. I had two teammates to help me push off in the four-man team...but I was alone in the two-man. This caused a major problem with my knee. When we arrived in Calgary, Wolfgang had almost completely recovered, but my injury had worsened."

A few days before the two-man competition, the two friends met.

"It was a very sad meeting. I told Wolfgang that he would have a better chance of winning the two-man gold medal if I were replaced," Schauerhammer said. "It was difficult for him to accept my decision because we had been planning and training together for four years. On a personal level, Wolfgang felt that he was responsible for my injury."

Hoppe tried to dissuade Schauerhammer but finally realized his friend's decision was final. Schauerhammer was replaced by Bogdan Musiol, a member of the four-man team.

When the four runs were completed, Hoppe and Musiol finished second behind the Soviet Union, losing by less than a second.

Wolfgang Hoppe (driving) and Dietmar Schauerhammer (far right, running) were reunited in the four-man event in Calgary.

"After the race, the press continually asked me if we would have won had I been Wolfgang's partner," said Schauerhammer. "Instead of asking that question, they should have written of the courage Wolfgang showed. You must remember, just two weeks before the race, we did not know whether Wolfgang would compete. In a sport where timing, teamwork, and practice are essential, when hundredths of a second separate gold from silver, you realize that a second place finish should be honored, not questioned."

Five days later, the finals for the four-man event were scheduled. Wolfgang Hoppe would attempt to become only the third man in history to win back-to-back gold medals in the bobsled event.

As the teams went through their last-minute preparations before the start of the race, the East German team held a dramatic meeting. One of the team members was Dietmar Schauerhammer.

"During the five days between the two-man and the four-man events, my leg was getting stronger," Schauerhammer said. "Wolfgang came over to me and said he would personally be pleased if I would join the four-man team. I thought for a moment and then told him, 'I think I can do it.' I took my position as the third man in the sled."

The competition got under way. After three runs, the East Germans were in second place and in a good position to win the gold medal. They trailed the first place Swiss team by $16/100$ of a second.

Hoppe's team turned in a magnificent final run, guaranteeing them at least a silver medal, with the Swiss the only team that could beat them for the gold— but only if they could stay within $16/100$ of a second of Hoppe's final run.

At the bottom of the course, the East Germans waited at the finish line as the Swiss started their run. The split times flashed on the scoreboard as the red sled came hurtling down. They were moving slower than Hoppe's team did in their previous run, but just barely. One miscalculation and the gold medal would go to the East Germans.

The Swiss crossed the finish line, and the scoreboard flashed the time. They had defeated the East Germans by $7/100$ of a second.

When it was over, Hoppe embraced his friend Dietmar Schauerhammer.

"For a few minutes we did not talk. We had lost by a blink of an eye," said Schauerhammer many years later. "Then I thanked Wolfgang for letting me join the team. He paused for a second and said, 'We've been together for a long time. It is better to win a silver medal with you on the team, than to win the gold medal without you.'"

Goalie Jimmy Foster (left) led the British team's assault on Canada's hockey dynasty.

THE FIRST GREAT HOCKEY UPSET

Most people believe that the greatest upsets in Olympic hockey history took place in 1960 and 1980, when the United States defeated the Soviet Union in crucial games before going on to win gold medals. So incredible were the American victories that they were given nicknames: the Team of Destiny in 1960 and the Miracle on Ice in 1980.

As spectacular as these upsets were, however, many consider Canada's loss at the 1936 Garmisch-Partenkirchen Games to be the greatest upset ever.

In their four previous gold medal victories before 1936, the Canadians had been awesome, never losing a game. As they plowed through the opposition, they created statistics so fantastic that they appeared to be misprints.

The first Olympic ice hockey competition took place at the 1920 Summer Games in Antwerp, joining figure skating on the program. Canada easily won the gold medal, scoring 29 goals in three games while holding the opposition to a total of one goal.

At the 1924 Games in Chamonix, the Canadians won five straight games, scoring a total of 110 goals to the opposition's three. Three of their winning scores were so high, they appeared to be football scores: They defeated Czechoslovakia 30–0, Sweden 22–0, and Switzerland 33–0. In the championship game, the United States won a moral victory by scoring a single goal before going down to a respectable 6–1 defeat.

Four years later, in St. Moritz, the Canadians again went undefeated, leaving their opponents unable to score a single goal, while Canada scored a total of 38.

At the 1932 Lake Placid Games, Canada went through all six games without a loss, scoring 32 goals to four for the opposition. In four Olympics, the Canadians had amassed a total of 209 goals while holding the opposition to a total of eight.

As the 1936 Games approached, eligibility questions surrounded the hockey competition, a controversy that would decide the winner of the gold medal. In 1935, Jimmy Foster of Canada, considered the greatest goaltender in amateur hockey, had moved to Great Britain. He offered to be the goaltender on the British team, and the Brits were thrilled to accept.

Although born in Glasgow, Scotland, Foster had moved with his family to Canada when he was a child. Foster excelled as a goaltender, and once held the incredible record of shutting out opponents for 417 straight minutes—the equivalent of almost seven straight games.

Foster's defection was just one of the political problems embroiling the Commonwealth. Eight other members of the British team had played all their hockey in Canada, and moved to Britain just before the Olympics. But they had made their move without getting permission from the Canadian Hockey Association.

The Canadians protested to the International Ice Hockey Federation, which agreed with them. For a time, the British team was in limbo. Finally, the Canadians withdrew their protest, taking the position that they had made their point—not expressed was the fact that the Canadians were certain they would win the gold anyway.

This would turn out to be a major miscalculation. The Canadians steamrolled their first three opponents by the usual lopsided margins, but when they met Great Britain in the semifinal, Foster held them to a single goal. The teams were deadlocked at 1–1 when Edgar Benchley of Great Britain scored in the final minutes to hand Canada its first ever Olympic loss, 2–1. Great Britain went on to win the gold medal with a record of five wins and two ties—the only unbeaten team in the competition. Goalie Jimmy Foster was the star, allowing a mere three goals in seven games.

A member of the British press, however, voiced his criticism of his country's only gold medal at the 1936 Winter Olympic Games: "By no stretch of the imagination is it fair to speak of a triumph for British ice hockey. One is ready to congratulate the players, but if the circumstances are considered impartially, it is difficult to feel enthusiastic over the success as one that belongs to Great Britain. Canada, champions until yesterday, was easily the best team and probably could beat Great Britain nine out of 10 times. Canada in truth has lost the title under its own name and won it under the name of Great Britain."

The writer was probably correct. Since its 1936 victory, Great Britain is yet to win a medal in Olympic hockey competition.

KARIN KANIA

When the 1988 Calgary Games approached, it was predicted that Karin Kania of East Germany would dominate the women's speed skating competition. This would be her third Olympics, and she was already a legend, the winner of three gold and two silver medals in her two previous Olympic competitions.

Kania began her career as a figure skater, but she grew too tall, so she switched to speed skating. And, at 5 feet 9 inches, she is one of the tallest speed skaters ever to compete on a world-class level.

"In speed skating, there's not an ideal size," Kania said. "The most important part of speed skating is whether one can effectively use one's stride in proper relationship with one's height, weight, and strength."

Comparatively unknown as an 18-year-old in 1980, Kania qualified for the East German team as an alternate. But a week before the Lake Placid Olympics, she won the World Sprint Championship and was immediately given a regular spot on the East German team. Then, in the Olympic 500 meters, she easily defeated the field. In a sport in which victory and defeat are decided by hundredths of a second, Kania was almost half a second faster than the second place finisher, Leah Mueller of the United States.

Four years later, Kania entered all four events at the 1984 Sarajevo Olympics, winning the 1000- and 1500-meter gold medals and the silver in both the 500 and 3000 meters.

"Before the 1988 Calgary Games, the press was extravagant in their predictions," Kania recalled. "Many stories talked about me winning four gold medals. Whenever I was asked about that, I would always reply that it was a possibility, but I would be very happy to repeat my Sarajevo victories in the 1000 and 1500 meters, for they were my specialties."

Kania's first race was the 500 meters, an event in which she had already won a gold and a silver, in 1980 and 1984.

Before Kania skated in the fifth pair, the world record had already been broken twice. Teammate Christa Rothenburger, the defending Olympic champion, broke her own world record in the second pair to take the lead. Ten minutes later, in the fourth pair, Bonnie Blair of the United States surpassed that world mark.

Kania had an opportunity to make Olympic history—to become the only woman to win the 500-meter event twice.

She skated a beautiful race, more than 2 1/2 seconds faster than when she had won the gold medal eight years earlier. But it was not fast enough. She finished third behind Blair and Rothenburger. Incredibly, only 14/100 of a second separated first and third places.

The next evening, the 3000 meters was scheduled, 7 1/2 times around the 400-meter oval. By the luck of the draw, Kania would skate against her teammate, defending champion Andrea Ehrig, in the fifth pair.

"Skating first has both advantages and disadvantages," Kania said. "If we skated fast enough to set a world record, it would certainly psychologically affect the skaters who followed. The disadvantage is miscalculating the pace, skating too fast in the beginning and leaving no energy for the finish."

The two teammates skated at an incredible pace.

"I had been suffering from a bad cold and cough," Kania said. "Although I was ahead of Andrea with two-and-a-half laps to go, I was exhausted. I had no feeling in my legs. I did not know whether I could finish the race."

Kania did finish, but she collapsed on the ice, not knowing that her teammate had broken the world record by four seconds. But that time did not hold up. Three pairs later, Yvonne van Gennip of the Netherlands beat Ehrig's time by 15/100 of a second to win the gold medal.

As the crowd cheered van Gennip's performance, Kania was still lying at the side of the track.

"It was the most frightening time of my life," she recalled. "I did not think I could ever stand up again."

Three days later, the final of the 1000 meters was scheduled. Kania had almost recovered from her cold. The 1000 meters was one of her favorite events—she was the defending champion and world record holder.

In her pair, Kania immediately demonstrated her courage. She broke her own world record and moved into first place.

"The only remaining skater with the speed to challenge me was my friend and teammate Christa Rothenburger," Kania recalled. "I watched her race, and when the times were flashed I was very surprised. They were faster than mine and faster than she had ever skated before."

When Rothenburger crossed the finish line, she had defeated Kania by 5/100 of a second to win the gold medal.

"I was happy for Christa, but to lose by such a small margin was very disappointing," Kania remembered. "That race has remained in my memory. I have relived it many times, wondering on which of the turns I could have been more technically correct. Five-hundredths of a second is less than a blink of an eye."

On Saturday, February 27, the 1500-meter final was scheduled. Kania was again the defending Olympic champion and world record holder.

In the fourth pair, she skated faster than all the previous skaters but more than 1 1/2 seconds slower than her world record. A little later, her time was beaten by the Netherland's Yvonne van Gennip by $^{14}/_{100}$ of a second.

"When I stood on the awards podium after the 1500 meters, it was very emotional for me," Kania said. "I knew this was my last Olympic race. My ambition was to close my career by defending my championships in the 1000 and 1500 meters. In those two races, I lost by a total time of 19-hundredths of a second."

Though her hopes were not realized, Karin Kania still made Olympic history by winning more medals than any other speed skater, male or female—three gold medals, four silver, and one bronze.

ALBERTO TOMBA

Before the Lillehammer Games began in February 1994, 27-year-old Alberto Tomba of Italy was asked by a journalist why he was the most sought-after athlete of the Games.

"Oh, there are many reasons," said Tomba. "Maybe because I am always smiling before the race and after the race. I'm always the same person. I always give a party after the race whether I have won or lost."

Tomba would have been considered outrageous if he hadn't been so good. His offhand remarks often became headlines on sports pages around the world. After one victorious race, he told the press, "I am the new messiah of skiing."

When asked to compare himself to the legendary Ingemar Stenmark of Sweden and Pirmin Zurbriggen of Switzerland, Tomba frowned.

"I don't want to become like them," he said seriously. "I'm considered a clown because I cannot be serious. But I'm afraid if I become more serious, I will stop winning."

One skier who faced Tomba over the years had an explanation for his ability.

"To be a good racer today, you must be able to turn off the brain and go on instinct," said Erwin Stricker, a former Italian star. "For that reason, Tomba will win a lot of races."

Regardless of why he wins, no one on the international sports scene has had a nickname like Tomba la Bomba, which literally means that Tomba explodes down the course like a bomb.

Tomba began his Olympic career at the 1988 Calgary Games. Leading to Calgary, he had won seven out of 10 World Cup starts in the slalom and was closing in on Stenmark's record of six consecutive World Cup victories. His streak came to a crashing finish when, on his birthday, December 19, he fell in the giant slalom.

Two months later at the Calgary Olympics, Tomba went off the course on his first run of the super giant slalom and was disqualified.

But four days later, in the giant slalom, he put on two spectacular runs to win the gold medal. The first phone call he made after the victory was to his father, a wealthy textile merchant, who had promised Tomba a Ferrari if he won the gold medal. "Make it a red one," Tomba said a few seconds after saying "hello."

"When I competed in Calgary, it was fun for me," Tomba said. "I gave myself parties, and everyone was having fun. Being a celebrity was new to me, and I loved it."

Between Calgary and Albertville, Tomba had his ups and downs. The year after the Calgary Olympics, he gained a lot of weight and won only one race on the circuit. To reverse what was happening, he was given a new coach, Gustavo Thoeni, who at the 1972 Sapporo Games had won the giant slalom.

After recovering from a broken collarbone, Tomba returned to great form, winning six World Cup races leading to the 1992 Albertville Olympics and finishing second in the overall World Cup standings.

In Albertville, Tomba made Olympic history when he won the giant slalom, becoming the only alpine skier to win gold medals in the same event in consecutive Olympics. A few days later, he won the silver in the slalom, missing the gold medal by $28/100$ of a second.

Tomba had become an international celebrity both on and off the slopes. He was photographed as much on the social scene as in competition. There were stories that Hollywood beckoned.

As the 1994 Lillehammer Games approached, the same rumors that had dogged his career were again circulating—that he was overweight and not paying attention to his training.

But to those in the press and public who loved him, he could do no wrong. They expected him to make more Olympic history in Lillehammer.

"It is true he is not training like the others," said a respected ski coach. "He's completely different from other skiers. Alberto is a free spirit. He is the best because he is a free spirit."

"You know, when I go to the other countries," Tomba remarked before leaving for Lillehammer, "everyone likes me and writes nice things about me. But at home in Italy, it is very difficult because every time I do something wrong, they write about it. Even if I do something right, they always say something in the newspapers the next day that is usually not true. When I started my Olympic career in Calgary, everything was fun and jokes. But it is all different. It is not so nice."

In Lillehammer, Tomba was the pre-race favorite in the giant slalom because of his two previous Olympic victories in that event. He was in 13th place after the first run and knew he would have to abandon caution on the second run.

He charged down the course with hopes for a medal, but he missed the third gate from the finish and was disqualified.

Four days later, the final day of the Lillehammer Games, the slalom was scheduled. By the luck of the draw, Tomba was the first competitor in the opening run. He would be the pathfinder in an event that had 60 competitors. He had the opportunity to become the only alpine skier in history to win gold medals in three successive Olympics.

Tomba navigated the course without mishap, but it soon became evident that he was not skiing very fast. At the end of the first run, Tomba was in 12th place, almost two seconds behind the leader, Thomas Stangassinger of Austria.

"Being first man down the course was not good for Alberto," commented his coach, Gustavo Thoeni. "He made mistakes, and he was frightened, which is not like him. I told him between rounds, 'You must go all out. You must go for broke,' as the saying goes."

The top 15 skiers went off in reverse order for the second run. Tomba, in 12th place, went fourth.

His second run was spectacular. He was the only man to go the distance in less than one minute. He found himself in first place, but there were still 11 men who could beat him.

"I did not think there was a chance for a medal," he recalled. "If there were two or three skiers ahead of me, maybe there was a chance. But 11 skiers...I did not think so."

Tomba's total score held up for the next 10 skiers. He was still in first place with only the first-round leader, Stangassinger, in a position to beat him.

Tomba waited at the bottom of the hill, watching the scoreboard and Stangassinger. When the Austrian crossed the finish line, he had defeated Tomba by $^{15}/_{100}$ of a second.

Alberto Tomba endeared himself to the world when he rushed over to embrace Stangassinger...in what may have been Tomba's last Olympic race. If it is, he will have left the arena with a record of three gold and two silver medals.

After Tomba's second place finish in the slalom, one columnist wrote: "Alberto's second run brought back the glories of the past. In less than one minute, he left a legacy for all those who will follow him. Truly, Alberto proved that a man is not finished when he loses, he is only finished when he leaves the arena."

GUNDE SVAN

Gunde Svan of Sweden is considered by many to be among the top cross-country ski racers in Olympic history. He lives in the small village of Vansboro, 250 kilometers northwest of Stockholm.

At the 1984 Sarajevo Olympics, 22-year-old Svan competed in all four men's events and stood on the awards podium four times, the winner of two gold medals, one silver, and one bronze.

As the 1988 Calgary Games drew near, many predicted that he would repeat his Sarajevo performance. Some even believed that this time he would stand on the top step of the podium after every race.

"You don't compete in ski racing to finish second or third," Svan said confidently. "You compete to win. If I don't win, I feel lousy."

Ironically, one of the great influences on Svan's career was an American, Bill Koch, whose silver medal in the 30 kilometers at the 1976 Innsbruck Olympics is the United States' only cross-country skiing medal to this day.

"Gunde and I became good friends when he was 13 years old," Koch said, "and we've remained good friends through the years. Gunde has everything. He has a tremendous amount of drive plus an incredible amount of natural ability. And he's so big and strong. When he takes a step, it's a big step. When he takes a stride, it's a big stride."

Svan's first race was the 30 kilometers. By the end of the first 10 kilometers, it became evident that this was not the same Svan who'd won the bronze medal four years earlier. He was in 12th place, 40 seconds behind the leader.

As the race continued, his position deteriorated. At 20 kilometers, he was more than two minutes off the leading time. At the finish, Svan was in 10th place in the most disappointing race of his Olympic career.

Four days later, Svan was confident that he could win the 15 kilometers. He was the defending champion and had an excellent starting position. He would start 84th in a field of 92 and thus would be able to gauge the times he had to beat.

But again, Svan turned in a mediocre performance. He finished 12th. There was depression in the Swedish camp as the skiers prepared for the 4 x 10-kilometer relay. Through two events, a Swede had yet to stand on the awards podium. All six medal places had been won by Soviet and Norwegian skiers, whom the Swedes would face in the relay.

Four years earlier, in Sarajevo, the Swedes had defeated the Soviets by 10 seconds, with Svan skiing a great anchor leg for the victory.

The Swedish strategy had changed for the Calgary relay. Svan would ski the third leg instead of the anchor. It was hoped that he would be able to break open the race during his leg, giving Sweden a large enough lead to hold off the final challengers on the anchor leg.

Svan's task would be a difficult one. He would be opposed by Mikhail Deviatiarov of the Soviet Union, who earlier in the week had won the 15 kilometers, the race in which Svan had finished 12th.

But it was a different Gunde Svan this time. He was now skiing with the strength that had been missing in his two previous races. At each checkpoint, his time was the fastest of the day.

When he finally passed off to his anchor teammate, Torgny Mogren, the Swedes were in front of the Soviets by 27 seconds. But the victory was not a certainty. Skiing the anchor leg for the Soviets was Alexei Prokurorov, who had earlier won the 30 kilometers. Still, the Swedish strategy was nearly perfect. At the finish, Mogren was 13 seconds ahead of his Soviet adversary.

Five days later, Svan was the 69th starter in a field of 70 in the 50-kilometer race, the most grueling competition on the cross-country program, a race of approximately 31 miles.

The relay victory had inspired Gunde Svan. At the halfway point, he was more than a minute faster than anyone in the race. He pressed on. Only a total physical collapse could thwart him.

At the 40-kilometer mark, with 10 kilometers left, Svan was almost $1\frac{1}{2}$ minutes ahead of his nearest competitor.

Finally, Svan entered the stadium, the finish line in sight. Cheers resounded through the stadium, for the spectators recognized the greatness of Svan's comeback since those first disastrous races.

When the awards ceremony finally took place and the Swedish national anthem was played in his honor, Gunde Svan knew he had finished his career with glory—winning four gold medals, one silver, and one bronze.

Irina Rodnina and Alexander Zaitsev, the most successful pair in the history of figure skating.

THE RUSSIAN INVASION

No country has dominated a Winter Olympic sport as has the Soviet Union in pairs figure skating. Russian skaters have won the Olympic gold medal nine straight times, from 1964 in Innsbruck through 1994 in Lillehammer. They have revolutionized the sport and catapulted the event into one of the most popular at the Winter Olympics, ranking it on a par with the individual men's and women's figure skating events.

The Soviets entered Olympic pairs figure skating competition for the first time at Squaw Valley in 1960. It could not have been predicted that the team finishing in ninth place, Lyudmila Belousova and Oleg Protopopov, would soon dominate the world scene. The married couple became known simply as the Protopopovs.

The Protopopovs won their first gold medal at the 1964 Innsbruck Games, and they defended their title in Grenoble four years later. Before their retirement, they had won two gold medals and four consecutive world championships (1965–1968), and had set the stage for young skaters in the Soviet Union to emulate their record.

The Protopopovs elevated pairs skating into an art form. They combined athleticism with ballet, and developed many of the lifts, spins, and twists that have become standard parts of today's pairs skating routines. Thunderous applause greeted their magnificent "death spirals," always the most popular part of their program.

The year after the 1968 Grenoble Games, the Protopopovs suffered their first defeat at the world championships after four successive wins. They were victims of their own success, for Lyudmila was already 33 and Oleg 36, and young skaters in the Soviet Union had been flocking to the rinks to attempt to rival the revered duo.

Coming onto the scene was the fiery 19-year-old Irina Rodnina and her 21-year-old partner, Alexei Ulanov. They would dethrone the Protopopovs and win three world championships in a row leading to the 1972 Games in Sapporo.

At the Sapporo Games, Rodnina and Ulanov skated superbly and won a close battle with another Soviet pair, Lyudmila Smirnova and Andrei Suraikin.

After being announced the gold medal winners, Rodnina left the ice in tears. Many believed they were tears of relief that the competition was over.

Ekaterina Gordeeva and Sergei Grinkov winning their first gold medal in Calgary.

But a few weeks later, after Rodnina and Ulanov had won their fourth straight world championship, her "victory" tears at the Olympic Games became headlines throughout the figure skating world. It was confirmed that Alexei Ulanov had fallen in love with Lyudmila Smirnova, the female half of the Soviet pair that had finished second at the Sapporo Olympics. The Olympic love story broke up the Soviet gold medal team, but it was well known in Soviet skating circles that Irina Rodnina was the superstar of the four skaters involved.

Soviet officials auditioned hundreds of skaters to replace Ulanov, who had paired with Smirnova, his future wife. Finally, young Alexander Zaitsev was selected to skate with Rodnina, and soon the pair developed into one of the great teams of figure skating history—rivaling their predecessors, the Protopopovs.

The new team of Rodnina and Zaitsev became inseparable on and off the ice. They married, and in two successive Olympics, they not only won gold medals but they also accomplished a feat that not even the Protopopovs had attained: In both their victories, they received all nine first place votes from the judges.

When the pair retired after the 1980 Lake Placid Games, Rodnina had tied a figure skating record that most thought would never be equaled. She had won three straight Olympic gold medals and 10 successive world championships— the same feat achieved by Sonja Henie almost half a century before.

Soviet pairs skaters continued to excel after the retirement of Rodnina and Zaitsev, winning the next four Olympic gold medals.

At the 1984 Games in Sarajevo, the Soviet pair of Elena Valova and Oleg Vasiliev won all first place votes to win the gold medal.

Two years later, there was another changing of the guard, and the beginning of another love story that would be one of the most dramatic—and tragic—in all of sport.

At the 1986 World Championships, a new pair emerged from the Soviet Union to challenge Olympic champions Valova and Vasiliev. They were 14-year-old Ekaterina Gordeeva and 18-year-old Sergei Grinkov.

The youngsters defeated the Olympic champions in both the 1986 and 1987 World Championships, then thrilled audiences at the 1988 Calgary Games, capturing all nine first place votes.

Though they lost to Valova and Vasiliev in the world championships following the Olympics, they came back to win the world championships again in 1989 and 1990. The two were now revered in skating circles, beloved by everyone...and in love with each other. They married and temporarily retired to have a baby.

The couple turned professional and were ineligible to compete in Albertville in 1992, but like many other pros, were returned to their amateur status to compete as part of the newly formed Russian team in the 1994 Lillehammer Games.

They were as magnificent as ever, winning their second gold medal. They won the world championships again the following year and were looking forward to the Nagano 1998 Olympic Games. But then tragedy struck. On November 20, 1995, during a practice session at Lake Placid, 28-year-old Sergei Grinkov collapsed and died from a previously undiagnosed heart ailment.

Two years before, Ekaterina Gordeeva had expressed to a friend what, in retrospect, turned out to be a premonition.

"Everything is too good," she said, "too perfect to last."

BILL KOCH

The combined total of gold medals won by American athletes at the Summer and Winter Olympics is by far the greatest of any country. But when 20-year-old Bill Koch of Guilford, Vermont, won the silver medal in the 30-kilometer cross-country race at the 1976 Innsbruck Games, it made front-page headlines throughout the United States. For in an event that had been dominated by skiers from Scandinavia and the Soviet Union, Koch is still the only American ever to stand on the awards podium. The best American placing before Koch's medal effort was 15th, 44 years earlier at the 1932 Lake Placid Games.

The 30 kilometers is a torturous event. For approximately 18 miles it taxes the strength, speed, and stamina of the skier. Koch bore an additional burden. He suffered from exercise-induced asthma—an ailment also afflicting Jackie Joyner-Kersee, America's two-time gold medal winner in the women's heptathlon. In order to breathe normally, Koch had to take medication that had been approved by the IOC.

"Before the race, I would have been happy to finish in the first 10," said Koch. "I had only raced the 30 kilometers twice in international competition before the Olympics."

Koch's appearance in Innsbruck owed much to the philosophy of his coach, Marty Hall, who had earlier been chosen to coach the American cross-country team at Innsbruck.

Coach Hall was a believer in the "youth movement," and the 20-year-old Koch fit the bill. Many perennial American team members were cut from the squad. One of the men eliminated from the team was Koch's mentor, Bob Gray.

"Bob Gray for years trained at Putney, my school, and he inspired me," said Koch. "When I was only a kid, he would take time from his own practice sessions and work with me. He would inspect my skis and give me helpful hints about my technique. He was truly my inspiration."

The day before the 30 kilometers, there was a major announcement that affected the race. The pre-race favorite, Thomas Magnusson of Sweden, had received news that his father had died. He immediately left Innsbruck to be with his family and would miss the race.

Once the race began, Coach Hall was full of confidence. "Nobody paid much attention to our cross-country skiers because we had never done well in the past," he said. "But we had a great month of training at Mount Telemark in Wisconsin, and I probably was the only one who knew what great condition our team was in."

Hall was right. No American journalists covered the event. They had all opted to watch either the men's downhill or the women's speed skating event, both of which were going on at the same time.

With Magnusson out of the race, there was no favorite. But Koch was confident. "You push yourself to the limit," he said, "and then all you can do is try and hold on."

Koch's run was spectacular, and he remained among the first five skiers most of the way. With seven kilometers left, he passed Coach Hall, who was stationed on the side of the course.

"I knew he was doing well as he approached me," said Hall. "I think a lot of the Europeans were puzzled that Bill was still up there."

When Koch crossed the finish line, news spread through the other venues in Innsbruck that an American had finished in second place behind Sergei Saveliev, a soldier in the Soviet military. It was nearly impossible to believe that Koch was less than 30 seconds behind the winner.

Koch was exhausted but ecstatic. The world press converged upon him, and he became the most sought-after athlete of the Games.

"There is a problem with winning a silver medal," Koch said. "Every question I was asked was, 'When was I going to win the gold?'"

Although Koch is most noted for his silver medal in the 30-kilometer cross-country, his fondest memory is from the 50-kilometer race that took place a few days later, where it appeared that he had a good chance of winning another medal.

He was leading all contenders after the first 30 kilometers, when he suddenly hit the wall. Total exhaustion set in, and he thought about quitting the race.

"I kept on falling farther and farther back in the field. Skiers I had passed earlier were now passing me," said Koch. "With five kilometers to go, I could barely move and there was a hill in front of me. I started up but was feeling faint.

"Then I felt a big hand on my shoulder; I was being pushed. I turned to see my idol, the magnificent Finn Juha Mieto. Juha is most famous for the 15K in Lake Placid, when he lost the closest ski race in history by one-hundredth of a second. But that day he showed me what sportsmanship and character truly are. He pushed me all the way to the top of the hill, and once there I got renewed spirit and energy. I went on to finish 13th. I'll never forget that. Never."

IRVING JAFFE

More than six decades ago, Irving Jaffe, the son of poor Jewish immigrants from Russia, lived in New York's Harlem and worked as a messenger on Wall Street for $16 a week. Being poor during the Depression was not unique. What was striking was the fact that Jaffe was going to present a serious challenge to the Scandinavians in long-distance speed skating at the 1932 Lake Placid Winter Olympic Games.

"My folks were immigrants and they didn't have their next nickel from one day to another," Jaffe recalled. "At the time, only rich kids could have enough money to go to the winter resorts, even to practice. We didn't have refrigerators in those days, so the only ice I saw was when the iceman with his tongs carried blocks of ice to our fifth-floor walk-up apartment."

The class system existed in those days. Rather than being jealous or feeling left out, Jaffe used it to his advantage.

"I didn't like the situation," said Jaffe. "It was difficult to watch these rich kids not having to work...getting their skates as gifts from their wealthy parents. But as I look back, if I was rich and it came easy, I might not have strived so hard."

On February 4, 1932, the opening day of the Lake Placid Games, eight athletes lined up for the finals of the 5000-meter speed skating event. One of the finalists was Irv Jaffe.

For the first time since the Winter Olympics began, in 1924, the North American rules of "pack racing" were put into effect in the speed skating events. This meant that all qualifiers from the preliminary races would line up against each other in one final race for the gold medal. In every other Olympics, it had been a race against the clock, with the gold medal going to the skater with the best time after a series of two-man heats. (At the 1992 Albertville Games, pack racing was re-introduced as an official sport under the name "short track.")

"The Europeans didn't like the change, but there is a certain fairness about it when the competition is outdoors," said Jaffe. "Everybody is skating under the same conditions. If the ice is soft, we're all skating on soft ice...not two at a time, which puts many skaters at a disadvantage. For example, if the heats are contested over two or three hours and the weather conditions change, fast ice can suddenly become slow ice."

Jaffe had good reason for his feelings. Four years earlier, at the 1928 St. Moritz Olympics, he had the fastest time in the 10,000 meters after all the main

Irv Jaffe is congratulated by silver medalist Ivar Ballangrud of Norway after winning his first "official" Olympic gold medal. At right is bronze medalist Frank Stack of Canada.

contenders had been on the course. Then the weather warmed and the ice softened, preventing a few skaters from making their attempt. The race was canceled.

"So I won, but if you read the record book, you'll find the word 'unofficial' in front of my victory," said Jaffe with a smile. "But at least the Europeans knew I was able to compete at their level."

In the 5000 meters at Lake Placid, the lead changed hands many times during the 12½ laps of the 400-meter oval. But this race of tactics was executed perfectly by Jaffe. Coming off the final turn, he overtook his countryman Ed Murphy to win the gold medal by inches.

Four days later, Irv Jaffe was one of the eight finalists in the 10,000 meters—25 times around the oval. Coming off the final turn, Jaffe led the favored Ivar Ballangrud of Norway, the world champion and pre-race favorite.

"I was coming down the homestretch," Jaffe recalled, "and I knew Ballangrud was close. But nobody was going to beat me on this day. I heard the crowd yelling and I could hear the sound of the other guy's blades. I was getting tired, but there were only a few meters left. So I dove across the finish and I knew no one was in front of me."

Jaffe lay flat on the ice just beyond the finish line, and from the stands, it appeared he was hurt.

"Six burly state troopers rushed to me and started to carry me off for emergency treatment," laughed Jaffe. "I started to laugh and they thought I was crazy...so I said, 'I'm OK guys...just a little tired. Just don't drop me.'"

ROSI MITTERMAIER

Before the 1976 Winter Olympic Games in Innsbruck, Austria, the tiny German mountain village of Reit im Winkl could be found on few maps. But just a few days into the Games, 25-year-old Rosi Mittermaier made her village internationally famous. In a major upset, she won the women's downhill skiing event—a surprise because in 10 previous World Cup seasons and two Olympic Games, she had never won a downhill race.

"When I competed at the 1968 and 1972 Games without winning any medals," recalled Mittermaier with a smile, "nobody even knew how to pronounce the name of my village. But when I won the downhill, everyone wrote about the 'famous' ski village of Reit im Winkl."

Three days later, after finishing second in the first run of the slalom, Mittermaier turned in a flawless second run, and her combined total time gave her a second gold medal.

"After the finish of the slalom, my teammates and hundreds of people came over to congratulate me," she recalled. "I began looking for my parents, but I couldn't find them in the crowd. I began telling people, 'I want to find my parents...I want to find my parents,' but I could not find them. Afterward, my father told me he forgot about my victory and was only worried about my safety."

Two days later, Mittermaier would try to make Olympic history. If she won the giant slalom, she would become the only woman to win all three alpine events.

"The newspaper people again began to write funny things," Mittermaier said. "They made a big story about my being called 'grandma' by my teammates because I was 25 years old, the oldest on the team. There was one story that referred to me as 'the old lady of the Games.' I didn't think 25 was so old."

Eighteen-year-old Kathy Kreiner of Canada was the first racer down the course in the giant slalom—an event in which each skier gets only one run. She turned in a magnificent time and held the lead after the next three women had completed the course.

Rosi Mittermaier was the fifth skier.

"I was not nervous. Winning three gold medals was not important," Mittermaier said more than two decades later. "After my first victory, my feeling was, 'I have won my gold medal so now I will ski for fun.' Then after I won my second gold medal, my feeling was, 'Now I have two gold medals, and I am still going to ski for fun.'"

Two-thirds of the way down the course, Mittermaier's time was more than half a second faster than Kreiner's.

"Everything was going well and I was having fun," she recalled as if it were yesterday. "But in any race, one can make a mistake. Near the end of my run, I made a mistake. It couldn't be seen by the spectators who were cheering me on, but I could feel it. When I crossed the finish line, I knew I did not have a winning time."

Mittermaier was correct. The slight mistake cost her the gold medal. She finished second, $12/100$ of a second behind Kreiner.

"I still have wonderful memories of Innsbruck," Mittermaier said, smiling. "I had fun and came away with two gold medals and one silver. And there's one other thing—there are a lot more people who know where my village of Reit im Winkl is."

BIRGER RUUD

No ski jumper has had a more fabled career than Birger Ruud of Norway, born in the mining town of Kongsberg, 45 miles from Oslo.

Birger Ruud started his Olympic career at the 1932 Lake Placid Games, but he was not the most famous Ruud competing there. The name Ruud was already in the Olympic record book after his older brother Sigmund won the silver medal in ski jumping at the 1928 St. Moritz Games.

Sigmund Ruud was also the favorite to win at the 1932 Lake Placid Games but could only finish seventh. Instead, the duel for top honors was between 20-year-old Birger Ruud and another 20-year-old Norwegian from Kongsberg, Hans Beck. Beck had been having ski jump battles with the Ruud brothers since childhood, but their contest at Lake Placid would be the closest of them all.

During the first of two rounds, Beck broke the Lake Placid–hill distance record and took an early lead.

Birger Ruud trailed in second place, a full five meters behind—considered a nearly insurmountable distance. Beck thought his lead would be good enough and played it safe on his second attempt—too safe. His second leap was nearly eight meters shorter than his first.

"I knew on my second jump I would have to go all out," said Ruud. "My choice was simple: I would either extend my abilities too much and fall—or I would win the gold medal."

Ruud's second jump was superb. His flight through the air and perfect landing earned him important style points to go along with his distance, which was 5.5 meters longer than Beck's.

The combined distance for both jumps put Beck and Ruud in a virtual tie, with the outcome dependent on style points. But since they grew up on the same ski jump, their styles were nearly identical.

The judges deliberated for more than four hours. Finally, it was announced that Ruud had defeated his boyhood friend by a little more than one point.

Ruud's spectacular Olympic victory was just a harbinger of things to come. Two years later, he won the famed Holmenkollen ski jump competition on the legendary Oslo hill that is used only once a year.

"There is no feeling like the Holmenkollen," said Ruud. "There are more than 100,000 people watching and you hear this incredible roar as you come down the in-run. The sound is glorious—as if it's coming from heaven."

The year after the Holmenkollen victory, Ruud won the World Ski Jumping Championship, making him the favorite to retain his Olympic title at the 1936 Games in Garmisch-Partenkirchen. But the day after the Opening Ceremonies, Ruud attempted to win an entirely different discipline, the downhill slalom combined—a two-day alpine event. It was unheard of for the top ski jumper in the world to try to use entirely different skills to compete against downhill and slalom specialists.

"It was a surprise to the Europeans, who specialized in alpine skiing, to see a Norwegian enter their event," said Ruud. "It was an even greater surprise to them when I won the downhill by more than four seconds. However, two days later, I lost any chance of winning the gold medal when I fell in the first run of the slalom. I got up and finished, but I was 20 seconds behind the leader. I had a very good second run and was able to finish fourth overall."

The ski jump was the final event of the 1936 Games, and before Chancellor Adolf Hitler and his entourage, Ruud turned in two spectacular jumps despite extremely bad weather. His style points were nearly perfect, and history was made: Birger Ruud became the first ski jumper in Olympic history to win successive gold medals.

"I was in the prime of my ski jumping career and probably could have won a third gold medal, but it was not to be," said Ruud. "World War II started in 1939 and the 1940 Games were canceled. When the Nazis occupied Norway in 1940, they wanted me to compete in exhibitions, but I refused. So during the war they put me in jail."

The Olympic Games were renewed in St. Moritz in 1948, three years after the war ended. Ruud was 36 years old and a coach of the Norwegian ski jumping team.

The night before the competition was to begin, the ski jump area was beset with high winds. There was concern that one of the young, inexperienced Norwegian ski jumpers might be injured. It was decided that Ruud should replace him.

In one of the most spectacular climaxes to an Olympic career, Ruud got off two tremendous leaps, losing the gold medal to fellow Norwegian Petter Hugsted by less than two points, but winning the silver medal.

Today Birger Ruud's career remains the most dramatic in Olympic ski jumping history. In three Olympic appearances in 1932, 1936, and 1948, he won two gold medals and one silver.

TORVILL AND DEAN

It is rare that three newspapers, independent of one another, headline the front pages of their morning editions with the same words: PURE GOLD.

But that's what greeted readers throughout Great Britain on the morning of February 15, 1984, heralding the gold-medal performance of Jayne Torvill and Christopher Dean. The night before, the team had mesmerized millions throughout the world with a scintillating and revolutionary program that won them the ice dancing event at the Sarajevo Winter Olympic Games. So spectacular was their victory that it brought forth the gushiest of adjectives from columnists who normally refrain from such adulating prose.

Not since the great Protopopovs of the Soviet Union, who had performed two decades earlier, had a twosome received such unanimous acclaim. Queen Elizabeth herself immediately wired Torvill and Dean: "Many congratulations on your super performance, which I watched with great pleasure. Elizabeth R."

Her Majesty's response was not surprising, as it is common courtesy for royalty to respond to royalty. For Their Highnesses, or T and D, as they are affectionately called, had reached artistic heights never before attained and which, most believe, will never be again.

When the final tabulations were in, they received a perfect set of 6s from all nine judges for artistry and originality. In addition, they received three more 6s and six 5.9s for technical merit and difficulty.

The accolades poured in not only from the monarchy and the public but from fellow skaters as well—rare for a sport in which envy and jealousy abound.

"It was the most beautiful and emotional moment I have ever experienced," reported two-time gold medal winner Dick Button from his television commentary booth.

Another former world champion Bernard Ford had even higher praise: "Watching Torvill and Dean skate is like watching God skate."

It was expected that the pair would dominate at least the next two Olympics, but they turned professional and thought they'd left the Olympic arena forever.

But as the 1994 Lillehammer Games approached, a change in the eligibility rules opened the door for professionals to return to the Olympics. Along with gold medal winners Brian Boitano, Katerina Witt, and the Russian pair of Gordeeva and Grinkov, Torvill and Dean would return to Olympic competition after a decade-long hiatus. Wealthy and in their mid-30s, they wanted to prove that they were still the best in the world.

Ice dancing is divided into three parts: two compulsory dances that account for 20 percent of the final score, an original dance worth 30 percent, and finally, a free dance worth 50 percent—the discipline that usually decides the winner and which garnered Torvill and Dean their unequaled string of 6s at the Sarajevo Games.

Torvill and Dean were in third place after the compulsories but quickly moved into the lead on the second discipline—original dance—gathering eight first place votes from the nine judges. As the free dance approached, they were the odds-on favorite to win.

When they finished their free skating routine, the audience heralded them with a tumultuous standing ovation. But the audience does not vote, and to this day, the millions then watching are still trying to figure out how the judges almost unanimously turned their backs on the pair. The British skaters finished in third place behind the "rock and roll" performance of Russia's Oksana Grichtchuk and Yevgeny Platov, the gold medal winners. Russia's other pair, the world championship husband-and-wife team of Maya Usova and Alexander Zhulin, edged out Torvill and Dean for the silver.

Torvill and Dean were as shocked as the viewers.

"We couldn't believe how well we skated," Torvill said afterward. "The audience reaction made us happy and thrilled. The judges obviously did not agree."

When the tabulations for the free dance were finally announced, they received only one 6—and that was from the British judge.

History had been made with their loss: It was the first time in 14 years that Torvill and Dean had been defeated in a major competition.

TONI SAILER

Toni Sailer and Anderl Molterer of Austria were friends, teammates, and rivals as the 1956 Cortina Olympics got under way. They were expected to battle it out for top honors in all three alpine skiing events.

Although Sailer had completely recovered from a broken leg suffered a few years earlier, he was surprised by the greeting he received from some of his competitors when he arrived in Cortina.

"'How come you are here?' several skiers asked me as I stepped off the bus," Sailer said with a laugh. "I answered, 'Why shouldn't I be?' And they said, 'I thought you had a broken leg.' So I said as I grabbed my legs, 'See, my legs are here with me. They are here with me.' I think they were trying to psyche me out."

In the first event, the giant slalom, Molterer turned in a nearly flawless run and moved into first place. Many of the spectators assumed victory was his.

But, as Molterer himself said, "You never can be assured of anything until Toni Sailer finishes his run. His build is perfect for alpine skiing. Because his legs are so long, he is able to put more drive into them."

Molterer's lead held, and then it was time for Sailer's run. When Sailer crossed the finish line, the announcement of his time was met with disbelief. His run was more than six seconds faster than Molterer's. His margin of victory was so large that it left Sailer in shock.

"I couldn't believe it," Sailer said. "I was waiting for someone to tell me that the timing was not working. I thought I might have to do it again."

But his time was confirmed. Sailer's margin of victory is still the largest in the history of Olympic alpine skiing.

The duel between Sailer and Molterer in the slalom was expected to be closer, for the event was Molterer's specialty. But Molterer fell during the first of his two runs and was out of the competition.

Sailer turned in the fastest time on each of his two runs, and his combined total left the second place finisher four seconds behind. Again, he was concerned that his time was incorrect. But once more it was confirmed. In two events, he had won by a total of more than 10 seconds.

A few days later, he and teammate Anderl Molterer met again in the downhill. A few minutes before the event was to begin, Sailer broke a binding strap. Sailer's coach began to panic, fearing that Sailer might miss his starting time.

As the minutes ticked by, Sailer received another strap from the trainer of the Italian team.

"Things got pretty hectic," Sailer recalled. "My coach was slapping me on the shoulder and saying things like 'Don't be nervous...don't be nervous.' I wasn't nervous, but he was going crazy. He kept slapping me and saying, 'You'll make it, you'll do OK.' And I said to myself, 'If he slaps me on the shoulder one more time, I'm going to hit him.'"

Molterer got off a good run that earned him the bronze medal, but Sailer was again sensational. He overwhelmed the finest downhill racers in the world, winning by 3$\frac{1}{2}$ seconds.

Toni Sailer had done what most experts thought was impossible—winning all three alpine events. Even more, each of his victories was overwhelming, devastating the opposition.

Sailer returned to his home in Kitzbühel a national hero and received Austria's most distinguished medal, the Golden Cross of Merit.

Thousands of letters arrived each week from adoring fans, but today, more than four decades later, Sailer's name is little known outside Austria.

Twelve years later in Grenoble, Jean-Claude Killy duplicated Sailer's feat by winning all three alpine gold medals. Compared to Sailer's margins of victory, however, Killy's were close, two by infinitesimal parts of a second. Comparisons between Sailer and Killy are still made, but Anderl Molterer has no question as to who was the best.

"To me, there will never be anyone who can compare with Tony Sailer," Molterer said. "He was unbelievable. He was...he was the king."

THE 1960 UNITED STATES HOCKEY TEAM
THE TEAM OF DESTINY

The most famous ice hockey competition at the Olympic Games took place at the 1980 Lake Placid Games, where a young U.S. hockey team won the gold medal. The United States went undefeated, winning six games and tying one. Along the way, they performed what history has called hockey's greatest Olympic upset, their 4–3 victory over the heavily favored Soviet Union.

Almost forgotten, however, was a similar situation 20 years earlier at the 1960 Squaw Valley Games, when the American team was again given little chance for championship honors. The favorites to win the gold medal were the defending champions from the Soviet Union and a strong squad from Canada.

To the surprise of most everyone, the U.S. team won its first four games. However, this streak was expected to end abruptly in its fifth game against the heavily favored Canadians. But the U.S. team, led by goaltender Jack McCartan, turned back the Canadians in a thrilling 2–1 victory.

Two days later, the United States met the Soviet Union.

The Americans scored early in the opening period, but the Soviets scored twice before the period was half over. The Americans then tied the game at the end of the second period when Billy Christian took a pass from his brother Roger and slipped the puck past the Soviet goalie.

The Soviets attacked relentlessly during the entire third period, but goalie Jack McCartan turned them away every time.

Finally, the Christian brothers joined together as they had earlier to put the Americans ahead 3–2, and McCartan did the rest, making save after save to thwart the now-desperate Soviet team. When the final buzzer sounded, history had been made. For the first time, the United States had defeated the Soviet Union in hockey.

To win the gold medal, the United States had to beat Czechoslovakia in its final game.

The Czechs led the Americans 4–3 at the end of two periods. During the intermission between the second and third periods, the Americans were physically and emotionally exhausted. Then one of the greatest acts of sportsmanship in Olympic history took place.

The American team was shocked to see Nikolai Sologubov, the captain of the Soviet team, walk into their dressing room.

Trying to understand Sologubov's broken English, the Americans finally realized that he was suggesting that the team members inhale oxygen. They took his recommendation.

Now almost fully revived, the American team scored six straight goals in the final period, while goaltender McCartan held the Czechs scoreless. The United States won the game and with it the gold medal.

A bit of irony remains. The last man to be cut from the 1960 Team of Destiny was Herb Brooks. Twenty years later, Brooks coached the U.S. team to its only other gold medal in hockey at the 1980 Lake Placid Games, an equally incredible upset that became known as the Miracle on Ice.

CHRISTA ROTHENBURGER

Christa Rothenburger of East Germany is not universally known in the sports world. Yet she is one of the most versatile athletes ever to enter the Olympic arena—a world-class competitor at both the Winter and Summer Games. She participated in the 1980, 1984, 1988, and 1992 Winter Games as a speed skater and in the 1988 Seoul Olympics as a cyclist.

At the 1980 Lake Placid Games, when she was 20 years old, Rothenburger was a favorite to medal in both the 500 and 1000 meters but failed to place in either.

"I was very disappointed," Rothenburger said. "But it was my first Olympics, and I think I learned a lot from the experience."

Learn she did, for four years later, in Sarajevo, she redeemed herself by winning the 500-meter gold medal.

She was again a favorite at the 1988 Calgary Games but had to settle for the silver medal in the 500 meters, losing by $2/100$ of a second to America's Bonnie Blair.

However, a few days later, Rothenburger came roaring down the homestretch to win the 1000 meters, defeating favored countrywoman Karin Kania by $5/100$ of a second. Waiting to greet her at the finish line was her coach of 14 years, Ernst Luding.

The crowd cheered her as she took a victory lap. Then suddenly the cheering turned to tumultuous laughter.

"I saw Ernst at the finish line," Rothenburger recalled. "I was so happy, but I didn't expect what happened next."

"We were both so happy. She was smiling and waving to the crowd," Luding said. "I waited until she circled the track to skate over to her. My legs were weak from excitement. Actually, I could feel nothing. So I embraced Christa and then suddenly I found myself sprawled on the ice. It happened in front of everybody. It must have looked funny, but there was so much joy, it didn't matter."

What the crowd did not know was that Luding was more than Rothenburger's coach. Two months after the Calgary Games, they were married.

With two gold medals and one silver, Rothenburger easily could have retired a national hero. Instead, she would attempt to make Olympic history.

"When Ernst first started coaching me, he realized there was something missing from my training," Rothenburger said. "It was ceaseless and monotonous."

"To bridge the gap between speed skating seasons, we decided that Christa should train in cycling," Luding said. "In the beginning, we did not have ambitions for Christa to move into world-class cycling. She raced only in local meets to remain competitive and stay in shape. But soon we realized that she had special qualities in cycling—world-class qualities."

So finally, Rothenburger and Luding made a momentous decision. After eight years of winning East Germany's national sprint cycling championships, Rothenburger would enter the 1000-meter cycling event at the 1988 Summer Olympics and attempt to become the only woman in history to win gold medals at both the Summer and Winter Games.

More than a half-century earlier, at the 1932 Lake Placid Winter Games, Eddie Eagan of the United States had accomplished that feat as a member of the victorious four-man bobsled team. Twelve years before, Eagan had won the light heavyweight boxing gold medal at the 1920 Antwerp Olympics. There was one other difference: Eagan's victories had taken place 12 years apart. Rothenburger's attempts would both take place in the same year.

Rothenburger won all three of her preliminary cycling heats in the 1988 Seoul Olympic Games, as did Erika Salumae of the Soviet Union. The two would meet in the best-of-three final.

Rothenburger won the first race, but Salumae came back to win the second. The gold medal would be decided by the third and final race.

With 200 meters to go, Rothenburger was in the lead. Almost simultaneously, the two cyclists started their final sprints.

The crowd was roaring for Rothenburger, knowing how close she was to making Olympic history.

But it was not to be. With just a few meters left in the race, Salumae caught Rothenburger, winning by just six inches.

Ernst Luding was philosophical about the loss. "There's a saying we have in Germany," Luding says, "that shared pain is half pain. But with joy, the opposite is true. In our lifetime, we have been fortunate enough to share an abundance of joy."

Vegard Ulvang

VEGARD ULVANG AND BJØRN DÆHLIE

When Vegard Ulvang won the 30-kilometer cross-country race at the 1992 Albertville Games, with countryman Bjørn Dæhlie finishing close behind to win the silver, all of Norway rejoiced. The win ended a 16-year losing streak for Norwegian cross-country skiers, dating back to the 1976 Innsbruck Games. Before the Albertville Games were over, Ulvang and Dæhlie would turn in performances that had no equal in Winter Olympic history.

"Bjørn Dæhlie is not just a rival," Ulvang said. "He is also a close friend. We spend a lot of time training together. He's very careful with details, and he never enters anything he doesn't expect to win. Even in the evening when we play cards, he wants to win."

"I learned so much from Vegard Ulvang," Dæhlie said. "We are together more than 200 days a year, and we are as close as brothers."

Three days after they won their gold and silver medals in the 30 kilometers in Albertville, Ulvang and Dæhlie were back at the starting line for the 10 kilometers, a distance new to the men's Olympic program.

The 10 kilometers was a difficult event for the skiers, particularly Ulvang. A heavy snow fell during the entire race, but Ulvang had additional problems—halfway into the race, he fell and broke his pole. He skied another 500 meters before he was handed a new pole by a teammate not in the race.

With a little more than four kilometers left, Ulvang was fourth, but in the later stages of the race, he was magnificent. He won by almost 20 seconds over Marco Albarello of Italy. Bjørn Dæhlie finished fourth, 25 seconds behind Ulvang.

Two days later, the combined pursuit was scheduled: a 15-kilometer freestyle race with a staggered start based on the results of the previous 10-kilometer event. Ulvang's victory in the 10 kilometers meant he would have a 25-second head start over his teammate—the equivalent of more than 200 meters.

Dæhlie, the reigning 15-kilometer world champion, went all out from the start. Less than one-third of the way into the pursuit, he passed Ulvang and went on to win the gold. Ulvang held off two Italians for the silver.

After three events, Ulvang had won two gold medals and one silver, and Dæhlie a gold and a silver.

Three days later came the 4 x 10-kilometer relay, a contest for national pride—country versus country—with each member of a four-man team skiing 10 kilometers.

Norway trailed after the first leg, but Ulvang's second leg broke the race open. The Norwegians increased their lead on the third leg, and when Dæhlie started off for the last 10 kilometers, the outcome was no longer in doubt.

As Dæhlie came down the stretch toward the finish line, he was overjoyed—so much so that though he endeared himself to his Norwegian fans, he received some criticism from the press. As he neared the finish line, he grabbed a Norwegian flag from a spectator, turned around, and began skiing backward to the finish line.

"I was so happy, I felt I had to do something," Dæhlie explained. "I did not mean anything bad, like some of the newspapers said. But I must say that even my father came to me and said I should not have done that in front of all those people."

Four days later, the 50 kilometers was scheduled—the most torturous event on the winter program. Dæhlie was again the class of the field. He led the race from the start. When he crossed the finish line, he was almost a full minute ahead of the second place finisher.

Ulvang and Dæhlie had brought glory back to Norway. After three trips to the Olympics without a victory, Norway had won all five men's cross-country skiing events, and Vegard Ulvang and Bjørn Dæhlie had each won three gold medals and one silver medal.

Two years later, before the home crowd in Lillehammer, Dæhlie continued his amazing winning record. In the same five events, he won two gold and two silver medals to equal the men's Winter Olympic record of five career gold medals.

Ulvang was less fortunate. Recovering from injuries and depressed after the recent death of his older brother, he garnered a silver in the relay.

Bjørn Dæhlie

Bobsled team USA I at Lake Placid in 1932: Jay O'Brien, Eddie Eagan, Tippy Gray, and Billy Fiske.

BILLY FISKE

As the story goes, 16-year-old Billy Fiske of the United States, the son of a wealthy Chicago banker, was vacationing at Switzerland's famed St. Moritz resort during the 1927 Christmas holidays, a month before the 1928 Winter Olympic Games were scheduled to take place there.

One day, young Billy was introduced to Jay O'Brien, the chairman of the U.S. Olympic Bobsled Committee and a member of the team selected to represent the United States at the Olympics.

"I'd like to be the driver of your team," Billy said.

"How old are you, son?" O'Brien asked, smiling.

"I was 16 last summer, sir," Billy answered.

"Well, come back in four years and we'll talk," O'Brien replied.

"Well, sir," responded Billy, "what will I do with the bobsled my father gave me for my birthday?"

The story may be apocryphal, but it is a fact that a few days later, Billy Fiske was named the driver of the hastily formed USA II—a second American bobsled team that would vie for championship honors.

On February 18, 1928, history was made. Fiske drove USA II to victory, defeating his American teammates by a half a second.

There was an additional honor for Fiske. He was the youngest male to win a Winter gold medal, a record he held for the next 64 years. At the 1992 Albertville Games, ski jumper Toni Nieminen of Finland won the large-hill gold medal—when he was just one day younger than Fiske had been.

Twenty-year-old Fiske arrived four years later at the 1932 Lake Placid Games to defend his Olympic title. Again, two American teams were entered in the four-man bobsled event.

This time, Fiske was the driver of USA I, and he put together a foursome that was straight out of one of those fictional Hollywood sports films of the 1930s.

Returning to the 1932 team was 40-year-old Clifford "Tippy" Gray, a songwriter whose most famous work was the best-selling "If You Were the Only Girl in the World." Gray, like Fiske, was looking to win his second gold medal.

Fiske next convinced Jay O'Brien, still the head of the American bobsled committee, to join the team as brakeman. Although he was 48 years old, he'd won a silver medal four years earlier as part of USA I, which had finished second to Fiske.

But the fourth member of the Fiske team was the shocker. He was 34-year-old Eddie Eagan, a Yale graduate, a Rhodes scholar, and the holder of a law degree, who had gained international fame 12 years earlier at the 1920 Antwerp Summer Olympics.

When the Summer Games were renewed in 1920 after World War I canceled the 1916 Games, Eagan, the captain of the Yale boxing team, was considered one of the world's best amateur light-heavyweights. He made the Olympic team, went to Antwerp, and came home with the gold medal.

It appeared that Eagan's Olympic career was over until a momentous meeting took place 12 years later.

"One day he came rushing home," remembered Peggy Eagan, Eddie's wife, "and said, 'Guess what? I'm on the U.S. bobsled team.' I thought that was pretty strange, because Eddie had never been on a bobsled before."

Incredibly, Billy Fiske quickly made experts out of his diverse crew, and after the four runs were completed, Fiske again was Olympic champion.

The victory was historic for more than one reason: Fiske and Gray had each won their second gold medals. And Eagan created a record that still stands today—he is the only athlete, male or female, to win gold medals in both Summer and Winter Olympic events.

The foursome never competed together again, but eight years later, Fiske went on to establish another first, though it was a tragic one.

During the summer of 1940, in World War II's Battle of Britain, Fiske served as a fighter pilot with the Royal Air Force—more than a year before the United States entered the war after the Japanese attack on Pearl Harbor.

After shooting down several planes, Fiske was badly burned when his engine was hit during a dogfight.

Though he managed to land his plane, he died the next day. In life, Billy Fiske was a man of many firsts. So, too, in death—he was the first American pilot to be killed in World War II.

GILLIS GRAFSTRÖM

Gillis Grafström of Sweden was an architect, a poet, and a painter. He was also the greatest gold medal winner in men's Olympic figure skating history—the winner of three straight championships, in 1920, 1924, and 1928.

Skating in an era that overlapped the career of the legendary Sonja Henie—also the winner of three successive Olympic gold medals—Grafström remains almost totally unknown except to devotees of Olympic trivia. Yet those who know of him believe he revolutionized men's figure skating as much as Sonja Henie did women's.

Grafström left the figure skating scene long before the advent of television. Unlike Henie, whose skating prowess and magnetic personality remain vivid today thanks to her starring roles in Hollywood motion pictures, only scratchy bits and pieces of primitive newsreels remain to attest that Gillis Grafström did exist.

"I was a lover of the arts," Grafström once said. "It is my desire to transpose those feelings to my performance. For I truly believe that skating is an art form."

In 1912, at age 19, he began his career, coming in second at the Swedish National Championships. A few years later, he would achieve national prominence, winning Swedish titles in 1917, 1918, and 1920.

Grafström's love of music was easily recognized in his routines. He skated to waltzes, tangos, and other music of the day, constantly inserting combinations of jumps and spins that skaters of the era eagerly imitated.

When the Summer Olympic Games were revived in 1920 in Antwerp after an eight-year hiatus because of World War I, men's and women's figure skating formed part of the program. This was a unique experiment, for the first official Winter Olympic Games would not take place until four years later in Chamonix.

Twenty-seven-year-old Gillis Grafström was overjoyed. His participation in the Antwerp Games was the beginning of his own personal love affair with the Olympics.

"I never thought it necessary to compete in the European championships or any of the others," said Grafström. "To me, the Olympic Games were the only real contest that symbolized who was the best in the world."

Grafström's performance in Antwerp was superb. All seven judges placed him first, and he took the top position on the awards podium.

Four years later, 30-year-old Grafström marched with the Swedish team in the Opening Ceremonies at the Chamonix Olympic Games. His appearance there began a rivalry with Willy Bockl, the great Austrian champion.

Grafström again was nearly perfect, gaining four first place- and three second place votes from the seven judges. Bockl garnered only two first-, four second-, and one third place vote. It did not go unnoticed that one of Bockl's first place votes was from the Austrian judge. Unfortunately for Grafström, none of the seven judges was Swedish, or victory might have been easier.

Grafström would again meet Bockl, at the 1928 St. Moritz Olympics. Suffering from a badly swollen knee, Grafström nevertheless skated through the pain, with a scintillating performance. Bockl was spectacular, with a series of jumps and spins that captivated the crowd. But only two of the judges gave him top honors. When the final scores were tabulated, Grafström had defeated his adversary by one point and earned his third straight gold medal. But his victory was overshadowed by a young 15-year-old Norwegian girl, Sonja Henie, who was besieged by the press after winning the women's figure skating gold medal.

"Even though I am 38 years old, I still have the great love for my sport that I had when I began," said Grafström, responding to reporters when asked why he would try again at the 1932 Lake Placid Games. "I am healthy and in good shape. There is no reason why I cannot win a fourth gold medal."

But it was not to be. The contest became a competition between the old and the young—38-year-old Gillis Grafström and 22-year-old Karl Schafer of Austria. Youth won out, and Grafström had to settle for the silver medal.

In addition to making mistakes that had been foreign to him in the past, Grafström also had to overcome a slight bump with a photographer during his routine. For the first time in his Olympic career, Grafström would not stand on the top step of the awards podium.

Gillis Grafström died in 1938 at the age of 44, but he still holds two men's figure skating records—he's the only man to win three gold medals and the only athlete, male or female, to win gold medals at both the Summer and Winter Games in the same event.

Christine Goitschel (left) and her sister, Marielle.

THE GOITSCHEL SISTERS

On January 29, 1964, almost 1,100 athletes representing 36 countries marched in the Opening Ceremonies of the ninth Winter Olympic Games in Innsbruck, Austria.

Two members of the French alpine ski team were sisters—18-year-old Marielle and 19-year-old Christine Goitschel. Before the Games would end, the sisters would make Olympic history, competing in two of the most dramatic races ever.

"My sister Christine and I, along with the American Jean Saubert, were the favorites in the slalom," remembered Marielle. "But Christine and I had a great incentive to win. No French woman had ever won an individual gold medal at the Winter Olympics."

The fastest combined time after two runs would determine the winner.

"I was in front after the first run," recalled Marielle. "My sister Christine was second and Jean Saubert fourth. I would ski last in the second round."

On her second run, Christine was magnificent. She went into the lead, almost 1 1/2 seconds in front of Saubert in second place. Marielle Goitschel was the only skier who had a chance to beat her sister.

"Almost as soon as she left the starting line, I could see that Marielle was not skiing recklessly," said Christine. "She normally attacks every gate, but I'm sure she skied a different race because I was in front."

Many years later, Marielle confirmed what her older sister had suspected.

"I left the starting gate with one thought," said Marielle. "To make no mistakes. With Christine in front, I wanted to make sure we each won a medal."

When Marielle finished her run, her combined total was almost a second slower than her sister's but fast enough to take second place ahead of Saubert. The Goitschel sisters had made Olympic history—becoming the first sisters to win the gold and silver medals. For Christine, there was an additional honor— she was the first French woman to win an individual gold medal at the Winter Olympic Games.

Two days later, the giant slalom was scheduled—one run down a treacherous 59-gate course. Again the favorites were the Goitschel sisters and Saubert.

Christine Goitschel was the first of the three to go down the course. Her run was magnificent—one minute and $53/100$ of a second—putting her in the lead.

Later, Saubert had an equally amazing run. Incredibly, her time was identical to Christine Goitschel's, to the hundredth of a second. If no one made a faster run, for the first time in Olympic alpine history the gold medal would be shared. And for the second time, Marielle Goitschel was the only one left who could defeat her sister.

"This time there was no question about how I would ski down the course," Marielle remembered with a smile. "There were only two possibilities: Christine and Jean Saubert would share the gold medal, or I would win it by myself."

A different Marielle Goitschel attacked the course, with the strength and speed that were missing two days before in the slalom. Halfway down the run, she was more than half a second faster than her sister and Saubert.

She continued down at breakneck speed. Only a fall or a major mistake would thwart her. When she crossed the finish line, she had the fastest time of the day by almost a full second.

For the second time in two days, the Goitschel sisters stood on the awards podium—now each had won a gold and silver medal.

Four years later, Marielle returned for the Grenoble Olympics at age 23. Again, she skied magnificently, winning the slalom, the same race in which she'd finished second to her sister four years earlier.

"I still think Marielle could have won the slalom in 1964," said Christine many years later. "I think maybe she gave me a gift. Nevertheless, I'm sure it will be Marielle whom history remembers as one of the greatest alpine skiers who ever lived."

MAGNAR SOLBERG

On February 12, 1968, 60 competitors representing 14 nations were preparing for the start of the 20-kilometer men's biathlon at the Grenoble Olympic Games. The 20-kilometer biathlon is a demanding event: Each athlete must cross-country ski approximately 12½ miles, stopping four different times to shoot at targets 50 meters away.

To win, an athlete must be a fast skier, as well as an accurate marksman, for he is required to shoot at five targets at each of the four stops along the route. For each missed target, a penalty of one minute is added to the biathlete's time.

One of the four biathletes competing for Norway in Grenoble was 31-year-old Magnar Solberg, a police officer from Trondheim. Of the four Norwegians, Solberg was the least experienced and the least known—even to his own team-mates. No one knew why he was selected, particularly since he had embarrassed himself in a pre-Olympic competition in Switzerland. His teammates would not have been upset if Solberg were back home in Trondheim instead of being part of the team in Grenoble.

But there was one person who believed that Solberg was world-class—his coach, Martin Stokken. "Martin Stokken was my superior officer in the police force," said Solberg. "He had great confidence in me. Through the years, he became my best friend, my coach, my second father."

"Very early, I was impressed by Magnar's strength under pressure," recalled Stokken. "One day during our police work, I was very hard on him, really yelling at him. Most people would have been intimidated, but Magnar was different. He did not flinch; he remained calm. Those are important qualities for the rifle-shooting phase of the biathlon. Since Magnar was a magnificent cross-country skier, I realized that he would be an ideal competitor for the biathlon."

In the summer before the 1968 Olympics, coach Stokken put Solberg through a rigorous training program of physical and mental tests. Since it was summer, Stokken devised a painful exercise to force Solberg to concentrate under the cold-weather high-pressure situations he would have to endure during the actual competition.

"I told Magnar to lie down on this anthill that was crawling with ants," said Stokken. "I then placed a target 50 meters away, the actual Olympic distance."

"The ants would crawl up my legs," said Solberg. "They were all over my face, everywhere. It was terrible, but Martin would not let me quit. At the time, I didn't

believe it, but my ability to concentrate under those conditions was far more stressful than the exhaustion I had to undergo during the competition."

In Grenoble, the favorite to win the gold medal was Alexander Tikhonov of the Soviet Union. He was the first man on the course, with the other contestants following at one-minute intervals.

As expected, Tikhonov set a very fast time, but along the way he picked up two penalty minutes by missing two targets out of his 20 shots.

Solberg was the third man out. Although he was traveling the course at a slower rate than Tikhonov, his pre-Olympic training masterminded by Stokken paid off.

He was one minute and five seconds slower than Tikhonov as he crossed the finish line, but his target shooting was perfect—20 hits out of 20 shots. Solberg was now in the lead by almost a minute.

Incredibly, his time held up even after each of the remaining 57 biathletes had finished the course. Magnar Solberg had won the gold medal. He also enjoyed the honor of being the only biathlete to have a perfect score at all 20 targets.

"When I stood on the awards platform as they played the Norwegian national anthem," recalled Solberg, "I knew that Martin Stokken had been correct in his training methods. All the anguish I suffered with the ants in the summer target practice had paid off in the shooting in Grenoble. Without Martin, I could not have done what I did."

Four years later, in Sapporo, 35-year-old Solberg was back to defend his title. Again, his greatest challenge was expected to come from Tikhonov.

But Tikhonov's hopes vanished at the first shooting range, where he missed three targets. Though Solberg missed two targets out of his 20, his overall performance was again the best of the 53 competitors. This time, he won the gold medal by a little more than 12 seconds.

"When I stood on the awards podium for the second time," recalled Solberg, "I thought of what an honor it was for my country. My thoughts again went to Martin Stokken. Later, when we met, we looked at each other silently. He rarely shows his emotions, but this time there were tears in his eyes, as there were in mine. It was then that we knew the years we had shared together were all worthwhile...just for these moments."

JOHANN OLAV KOSS

On February 8, 1992, speed skater Johann Olav Koss of Norway watched the Opening Ceremonies of the Albertville Olympics from a Bavarian hospital bed, where he was suffering from an inflamed pancreas. In less than a week, he was expected to compete in the 5000 meters, the first of his three events. Before his illness, it had been predicted that he would be a multiple gold medal winner, for at the world championships the year before he was the overall champion, winning three of the four events and setting two world records.

On February 10, Koss rejoined the team and three days later, though still weak, he was able to finish seventh in the 5000 meters.

Three days later, the fully recovered Koss amazed even himself by winning the 1500 meters, defeating countryman Adne Sonderal by 4/100 of a second.

In the 10,000 meters, although he was the world record holder, he finished second, 2½ seconds behind Bart Veldcamp of the Netherlands. Veldcamp's winning time was almost 30 seconds slower than Koss' world record.

Two years later, as the 1994 Lillehammer Games approached, rumors were circulating that Koss was again not in top physical shape. It appeared that Koss, the son of two doctors and himself a medical student, had not fully recovered from an injured knee.

"The story of my knee injury was made much bigger by the press than it actually was," said Koss. "I tried to keep it a secret among the team members, but the story reached the press anyway. All people kept asking me was, 'How is your leg?' My leg was perfect, but it was a better story if I was injured—just like in Albertville two years before."

Koss immediately proved that the press reports of his injury were unfounded. Skating in the fourth pair, he set a world record, defeating his countryman Kjell Storelid by almost eight seconds.

Three days after winning the 5000 meters, Koss stepped to the starting line for the 1500 meters. This was not his favorite event—he was ranked sixth in the World Cup standings.

The favorite in the race was Rintje Ritsma of the Netherlands, the world record holder who was expected to battle for the gold medal with his teammate Falko Zandstra.

Koss was at a disadvantage skating in the second pair. The two Dutch skaters would be in later pairs and would know the time they would have to beat.

Koss skated a magnificent 1500 meters, breaking Ritsma's world record. Competing before the two Dutch skaters turned into an advantage for Koss. Zandstra, skating in the fifth pair, and Ritsma, following him in the sixth, both had to change their tactics and go all out from the start. Each had a faster time during the early part of his race, but faded badly in the last lap. Koss had won his second gold medal.

As he stood on the awards platform, all of Norway rejoiced. Later, at a press conference, the whole world would rejoice. There Koss announced that he was giving his $30,000 bonus money from the Norwegian Athletic Federation to Olympic Aid, a charity formed to assist children in war-torn areas like Sarajevo, the site of the 1984 Winter Games.

"When I won my first medal, it was such a glorious feeling," said Koss. "So when I went to bed that night, I said, 'This is unbelievable, and if it happens again, I want to share it with someone—share it with the people who really need it.' This is very personal. And so my involvement with Olympic Aid gives me and all sportsmen a chance to give something back for what sport has done for us. So I really hope that what I am doing will help bring solidarity and peace to the world."

When he finished, even jaded reporters rose to their feet and gave him a standing ovation. In the superstar era of agents, lawyers, and public relations people choreographing their client's every movement, Johann Olav Koss had broken the mold.

Four days after his second victory, Koss prepared for his final Olympic race, the 10,000 meters. "I decided I would skate the 10,000 meters the same way I skated the 5000 meters," said Koss. "I would go all out from the start and hope for the best."

Koss's strategy had dual consequences—one positive, one negative. He was shattering his own world record at the halfway mark, but never in his career had he been so exhausted.

"The ice was fast, very fast," said Koss. "So I decided to go faster, and still I felt I was not going fast enough. The crowd was screaming and I said to myself, 'Wow, will I be able to finish?'"

Koss not only finished, but he also broke his own world record by almost 13 seconds and won the race by more than 18 seconds.

Johann Olav Koss finished his Olympic career by winning three gold medals in three events at the Lillehammer Games, setting a world record each time. But more than that, he had given back as much as he'd received.

MATTI NYKÄNEN

As the 1988 Calgary Games approached, ski jumper Matti Nykänen of Finland was considered an enigma.

Four years earlier, at the Sarajevo Winter Olympic Games, he had won the gold medal in the 90-meter ski jump and the silver in the 70 meters. Many believed him to be the greatest talent in the history of the sport, and it was almost unanimously predicted that he would win both events in Calgary.

But following Sarajevo, Nykänen's personal life placed his career in jeopardy. He had to overcome personal problems with alcohol, the police, the press, his teammates, and his lifelong coach, Matti Pulli. Nykänen's behavior was so offensive that he was twice thrown off the Finnish national team.

"After Sarajevo, my life was different," Nykänen said. "I am not happy with many things that happened, since all my activities were printed in the newspapers and talked about on television. However, when my son was born, it was the happiest time of my life, and I knew that I must change my style of living."

"Almost all of Finland loved him," Pulli said. "But he received so much acclaim when he was so young. He did not know how to handle it. Now he has changed. He's older and much wiser."

The 70 meters was the first of three jumping events in which Nykänen would compete at the 1988 Calgary Games. Before the two weeks were over, he would try to repeat his 1984 win on the 90-meter hill and then join three of his countrymen for the team championship.

Many people have misconceptions about ski jumping. For example, the terms 70-meter and 90-meter hill do not signify the height of the starting point. Rather, they describe the distance from the takeoff point to the normal landing area two-thirds of the distance down the hill. There is also an optical illusion for spectators. Once in flight, the ski jumper rarely soars more than 10 feet off the ground.

In the 70-meter competition in Calgary, Nykänen got off the two longest jumps of the afternoon. He leaped almost 294 feet in the first round to take the lead, and then came back in the second round with yet another jump of nearly the same distance to win the gold medal.

"Four years earlier, in Sarajevo, I had to settle for the silver medal in the 70 meters," recalled Nykänen. "Now that I had won the gold, I could look forward to repeating my win in the 90 meters."

The 90-meter competition was postponed twice because of high winds, which created dangerous situations for the jumpers.

"It was very stressful for all of us," recalled Nykänen, "but I was prepared for this. Your mental ability must be in unison with your physical capabilities in order to win."

When the weather finally became clear and calm, the competition got under way.

It became evident on Nykänen's first attempt that the delay did not affect him. He jumped four meters farther than any other jumper, a margin so great that only a disaster in the second round could deprive him of the victory.

When Nykänen soared through the air and landed perfectly on his second attempt, history was made: He had become the only ski jumper in history to win three gold medals.

The following day, a new Olympic event would take place—the team competition. Eleven teams of four men each would compete, with the three highest scores on each team counting toward the final score.

Once again, Nykänen was superb. His combined distances were by far the longest leaps of the afternoon, ensuring victory for Finland and earning him his fourth gold medal.

Nykänen was given a hero's welcome when he returned to his hometown of Jyvaskyla, 275 kilometers north of Helsinki. Thousands turned out to greet him.

To the Finns, Matti Nykänen epitomized the spirit and tradition of their homeland, bringing back memories of their great Olympians of the past: a heritage steeped in a philosophy centuries old, encompassing the love of the outdoors, the sun, the woods, and what the Finnish call *sesu*—unyielding courage, stamina, fortitude, and honor.

With his victories in Sarajevo and Calgary, Matti Nykänen joined his legendary countrymen—athletes who for all time will be revered as the Flying Finns.

After Hayes Jenkins (right) won the gold in 1956, brother David took over.

THE JENKINS BROTHERS

When 14-year-old Tara Lipinski of the United States won the 1997 women's World Figure Skating Championship, she upset the popular belief that you had to pay your dues before the judges would consider you for championship honors—meaning a skater had to do a lot of losing before earning a top place on the awards podium.

But if there was a pecking order in the past, the Jenkins brothers, Hayes and David, illustrated it, having spent many years paying their dues.

When Dick Button became America's first men's figure skating gold medal winner at the 1948 St. Moritz Games, 15-year-old Hayes Alan Jenkins was already showing signs that he could become Button's successor by winning his first national gold medal at the U.S. Junior Championships. The following year, he finished sixth at the senior world championships while still a junior.

But that was the era of Dick Button, and leading to the 1952 Oslo Olympics, Hayes Jenkins consistently finished behind the 1948 Olympic champion.

"Dick Button was a great skater, a dramatic influence for me," said Jenkins. "He brought athleticism to American skating, and that appealed to me."

At 18, Hayes Jenkins made the U.S. Olympic team in 1952, and finished fourth behind Button's second gold medal victory in Oslo.

"I thought it a great honor just to make the team, even though I was disappointed with not winning a medal," said Jenkins. "I was prepared at the time to retire gracefully from the sport and concentrate on my college education. But when Dick Button retired after the 1952 Olympics, I decided to skate one more year. Fortunately, I was able to win the 1953 World Championships. Then I guess the element of pride set in—and a little ego. I wanted to see if I could defend my world title."

Jenkins not only defended his title successfully but, in the period between 1953 and 1956, he also built a record that challenged Button's. Jenkins won four U.S. championships, three world championships, and two North American championships leading up to the 1956 Games in Cortina.

In Cortina, Jenkins became the odds-on favorite to succeed Button as Olympic champion. He was joined on the team by his own 19-year-old brother, David, and

Ronnie Robertson. The year before, Hayes Jenkins, Robertson, and David Jenkins won the gold, silver, and bronze medals in the world championships.

The same American trio made Olympic history in Cortina where, for the first time, one country swept all three men's figure skating medals. For Hayes Jenkins, it was the culmination of an eight-year odyssey—one that included practicing 40 hours a week, 10 months a year.

"There was a special pride for me standing on the victory platform in 1956," said Hayes Jenkins. "It was special because my brother David was on the podium with me, the winner of the bronze medal. It is something we could share throughout our lifetime."

Hayes Jenkins finished his career by winning his fourth world championship after the 1956 Games. Then the mantle was turned over to his brother David, who was almost three years younger. David Jenkins immediately showed that he was a worthy successor by winning the American, North American, and world championship titles the following year. In the years leading to the 1960 Squaw Valley Games, David continued to win championships, making him the favorite to again place the Jenkins name in the Olympic record book.

"I was more nervous watching the Olympics in 1960 than I was when I competed," said Hayes Jenkins. "I couldn't go to the Squaw Valley Games, but I had a double involvement. Of course, I was nervous for my brother David, but also for my girlfriend, Carol Heiss, who was competing in the women's event. It was agonizing waiting for the phone to ring to find out what happened."

The story had a Hollywood ending. David joined his brother as Olympic champion, and Carol joined the family, too, as the 1960 women's Olympic champion—and as Hayes Jenkins' wife.

CAROL HEISS

Twenty-year-old Carol Heiss of the United States was on a mission when she stepped onto the ice for the final of the women's figure skating competition at the 1960 Squaw Valley Olympics—to fulfill a promise she'd made to her beloved mother, Marie.

Four years earlier, at the 1956 Cortina Games, 16-year-old Heiss had won the silver medal, finishing second to teammate Tenley Albright. Marie Heiss, Carol's mother, though stricken with terminal cancer, had traveled to Cortina to witness the competition.

Two weeks later, Carol and her mother went on to Garmisch-Partenkirchen for the world championships. There, Carol stunned the skating world by defeating Albright to take top honors. It was the first of five consecutive world championships that Carol would win but the last Marie Heiss would attend. Marie died that October.

"I was thrilled that Mom was there to see me win the world championships," Heiss said. "But she instinctively knew I wanted something more. Later that year, Mom and I had one of our last talks. She knew the end was near. She asked, 'Carol, do you really want to become the Olympic champion?' And I said, 'More than anything else in the world.' Then Mom said, 'I won't be there, but don't let anything or anybody stop you from reaching your goal.'"

Marie Heiss was Carol's inspiration. In 1946, when Carol was 6 years old, her mother took her to the Skating Club of New York, where the famed French husband-and-wife team of Pierre and Andrée Brunet was preparing young skaters for future careers.

To be taken on by the Brunets would be a coup for any skater. They were Olympic legends after winning gold medals in the pairs at both the 1928 and 1932 Olympics.

When their careers were over, they settled in New York to train their son, Jean-Pierre, to follow in their footsteps. But their dreams for their son ended tragically when Jean-Pierre was killed in an automobile accident.

At the time, no one imagined that the meeting would be the beginning of a historic figure skating relationship.

"She seemed awfully young," Andrée Brunet said, "but she had a marvelous personality and seemed so dedicated at so early an age. While I was talking to

her mother, she stamped her foot a few times and said, 'I want to skate, I want to skate.' So I gave her the opportunity to perform for me."

Andrée Brunet was so impressed, she called in her husband to critique the youngster.

"Well, I watched her skate, and she was years beyond her age," said Pierre Brunet. "I quickly recognized that she had immense potential and could become a champion." That meeting in 1946 would turn out to be a momentous one for Carol.

"Pierre Brunet was the only coach I ever had," Heiss said. "He was like a second father. He became involved in my entire life...what I was wearing, my hairdo, what college was I going to, who I was dating."

Under the guidance of Pierre Brunet and the enthusiasm of her mother, Carol soon began winning championships, her first at the age of 11 when she took the U.S. Novice Ladies Crown. The following year, she won the Ladies Junior Championships, the youngest skater ever to win both crowns back-to-back.

Championship after championship followed, with Marie Heiss always in attendance.

"Mom was marvelous. She made going to practice fun," Heiss said. "I remember one Christmas Eve, I was looking forward to a day off when I could sleep late and not have to practice. Then Mom said, 'Carol, won't it be great tomorrow on Christmas Day? You'll have the ice all to yourself. You can train for five hours and no one will be there but us.'"

At the 1960 Squaw Valley Games, Heiss was magnificent. She captivated the crowds—and the judges even more. All nine officials gave her first place votes. When she returned home after the Games, she became the first American Winter Olympian to receive a ticker-tape parade in New York City.

Following her retirement in 1960, Heiss married Hayes Alan Jenkins, who had won the men's figure skating gold medal at the 1956 Cortina Olympics—the Games in which 16-year-old Heiss captured the silver.

Today, Carol Heiss has fond memories of those glory days when she won a silver and a gold medal in two Olympic appearances.

"I had the joy of wonderful people behind me...my mother, the Brunets," Heiss said. "They taught me that there is more to life than winning. What I remember most is that they gave me a fully rounded philosophy of life; that an Olympic gold medal cannot give you lifetime happiness—that you must go on to other things."

LEONHARD STOCK

On Saturday, February 13, 1988, more than 2,000 athletes and officials were greeted by 60,000 fans at the Opening Ceremonies of the Calgary Olympic Games. Given the honor of carrying the Austrian flag was downhill racer Leonhard Stock, who in one month would celebrate his 30th birthday. But Stock was not thinking of his birthday. Rather, his thoughts were on his race the following day. This would be his final Olympic downhill, climaxing one of the most dramatic careers in Olympic history, one that began eight years earlier, at the 1980 Lake Placid Games.

"We were very strong in the downhill in 1980, and it was difficult for our coaches to select the four-man team," recalled Stock. "The first big surprise came when Franz Klammer, who won the thrilling downhill four years earlier in Innsbruck, was not selected. Then another big surprise. Even though I was still recovering from a broken collarbone and torn ligaments in my knee, I was selected as an alternate in case one of my teammates was not able to compete."

In the week preceding the Lake Placid Games, Austrian officials held a series of races to make certain that the team members were in top shape and would be serious medal contenders.

"I performed very well in the trials," said Stock. "In two races, I had the fastest times not only against my teammates but against the competitors from all the other countries. This caused our coaches to reconsider the team. Finally, they decided I should be one of the four Austrians to compete in the downhill, and I replaced one of the original men selected."

The Austrian press wrote scathing articles concerning the snub to Klammer, a national hero, and the addition of the 21-year-old Stock, whose physical condition was still suspect despite his pre-Olympic performances.

On February 14, 1980, all that was put to rest in the downhill. Leonhard Stock, skiing ninth in the field of 47, turned in an amazing performance to win the gold medal. The man who was an alternate prior to Lake Placid had skied to the top step of the awards podium and would return home a national hero. Now, even his detractors were predicting another victory for Stock in four years' time at the Sarajevo Olympics.

"After winning the gold medal, I returned home to my family," said Stock. "My wife and I opened a ski hotel in Finkenberg. I continued to ski on the World Cup circuit, but in the years between Lake Placid and Sarajevo, I was not able to win a single race."

As the 1984 Sarajevo Games approached, the Austrian coaches were forced to make a decision similar to the one they had made before the Lake Placid Games. Like Franz Klammer before him, Leonhard Stock, the defending Olympic champion, was not selected for the team.

"I was of course disappointed," said Stock. "Many people in the press wrote that I should quit. But I could not imagine my life without skiing and competition. When one loves to ski and is healthy, then on any given day it is possible to win a medal, no matter what has happened before or what will happen after. So between Sarajevo and the 1988 Calgary Games, I trained very hard."

Stock's persistence paid off, and he was again named to the 1988 Austrian Olympic team.

After a one-day delay because of bad weather, 51 men gathered at the top of the nearly two-mile downhill ski course in Calgary for the start of the single-run event.

The favorites in the race were two Swiss—Pirmin Zurbriggen and Peter Mueller. But the sentimental favorite for many was Leonhard Stock.

Mueller was the first skier down the course, and he turned in a spectacular time—two minutes and $^{14}/_{100}$ of a second. Ten skiers would follow, but none could come close to Mueller's time. The 12th skier was Stock.

"I now realized that Peter Mueller had turned in an amazing run," recalled Stock, "particularly because he was the first man down the course."

Stock turned in a very fast run—not good enough for the lead, but fast enough to place him in second position, with a good chance to medal.

"My chance for a gold medal was over, but there was still a great opportunity for second or third place," said Stock. "I had not won a major race in eight years, and it would be rewarding to once again have one of the places on the awards podium."

The 14th skier down the course was Zurbriggen. He turned in the fastest time of the day—the only run completed in less than two minutes—and moved into first place. Mueller was now second and Stock third.

Stock waited at the bottom of the hill for the run of France's Franck Piccard, the last man who could keep him off the awards podium.

"The wait at the bottom of the hill was agonizing," recalled Stock solemnly. "You could see on the scoreboard the intermediate times of the skiers, and you knew how they were doing against you."

Piccard started down the course. His times at the checkpoints were not fast enough to challenge Zurbriggen and Mueller for the gold and silver medals, but he was still in the race for the bronze.

Finally, he crossed the finish line. Stock looked to the scoreboard. Piccard had beaten him by $^{32}/_{100}$ of a second. Leonhard Stock finished in fourth place.

"Of course I was disappointed that I did not win a medal," said Stock. "But that is life. I did what many thought I could not do. And that in a sense is also a victory. To do your best...your very best. And that is what I did, my very best."

MAURILIO DE ZOLT

On Tuesday, February 22, 1994, thousands of spectators lined the entire length of the 10-kilometer cross-country ski route outside of Lillehammer, Norway, to witness the men's 4 x 10-kilometer relay.

The race had particular significance for the host Norwegians, for it was a team event—four men each from 14 countries—and national pride was at stake.

The Norwegian team was the heavy favorite. They were the defending Olympic champions, and their foursome was composed of Olympic and world champions. Two years earlier, at the Albertville Games, they'd won all five cross-country skiing events. In Lillehammer, they had extended their unbeaten string with three straight victories. Now the Norwegian people fully expected the winning streak to continue, though there were some who believed that the Italian team could put up a good fight.

The relay is one of the few cross-country ski events raced not against the clock but head-to-head. Often, the outcome of the race is decided during the first 10-kilometer leg. Leading off for Norway would be Sture Silvertsen, the reigning 10-kilometer world champion. He was expected to give the Norwegians a commanding lead and set the stage for their superstars—Vegard Ulvang, Thomas Alsgarrd, and Bjørn Dæhlie—to bring home the victory.

Opposing Silvertsen on the opening leg for Italy was 43-year-old Maurilio De Zolt. In previous Olympics, De Zolt had won two individual silver medals. But in Lillehammer many considered him too old. Others believed that his selection for the relay indicated that Italian coaches had given up hope for the gold medal in the relay, and would settle for the silver or bronze. But Maurilio De Zolt was accustomed to such talk.

"I tried out for the national team when I was 27 or 28, and even then the coaches said I was too old. Then I started to win some races, and the officials decided that perhaps they were wrong."

De Zolt competed in his first Olympics in Lake Placid at age 29, though he finished no better than 20th in any individual event. Incredibly, at an age when many athletes start to deteriorate, De Zolt began to improve. He eventually won a silver medal in the challenging 50-kilometer event at the 1988 Calgary Olympics when he was 37, and another silver at the 1992 Albertville Games at age 41.

"People wondered how I'd lasted so long," said De Zolt with a laugh. "Well, I trained hard and believed in special food and drink—particularly pasta and a lot of good red wine. It's difficult to say how many glasses I'd drink—and if I told you, I would probably get in trouble."

But a year before the Lillehammer Games, De Zolt's performances were poor, and it was believed that his age had finally caught up with him.

As the relay got under way, Sture Silvertsen took the early lead, followed by Mika Myllyla of Finland. De Zolt fell back to fifth place but tried desperately to stay within sight of the leaders.

"Ten kilometers is not my favorite distance. I won both my silver medals in the 50 kilometers," recalled De Zolt. "The year before, at the world championships, I again skied against Silvertsen in the first leg, but I finished a minute behind him, and the Norwegians went on to an easy victory. I knew that in Lillehammer I must do better, or the result would be the same."

The first leg was a grueling one. Silvertsen and Myllyla battled inches apart for the entire 10 kilometers. But they could not shake De Zolt. In one of the most courageous performances of his career, De Zolt finished his leg a mere 10 seconds behind the front-runners. He had closed the margin between him and Silvertsen by a full 50 seconds from his effort at the world championships one year earlier.

De Zolt's gutsy performance gave new inspiration to the rest of the Italian team, in particular Silvio Fauner, who had the unenviable task of skiing the anchor leg against the magnificent Bjørn Dæhlie. Dæhlie had already won two individual gold medals in Lillehammer to go with the three he'd won two years earlier in Albertville.

The Norwegians, Italians, and Finns pulled away from the other teams during the second and third legs, and when Dæhlie, Fauner, and Jari Isometsa of Finland skied off for the final 10-kilometer leg, they were virtually even. The situation was almost a duplicate of the relay in Albertville. Then, Dæhlie had quickly left Fauner behind and won the gold medal by more than a minute. Now, to the thousands of Norwegian fans along the course, it was just a matter of time before Dæhlie would pull away to ensure another victory.

But it never happened. Isometsa fell off the pace early, but Fauner, in an inspired performance, stayed even with the Norwegian champion throughout. Then, with 100 meters left, Fauner passed Dæhlie on the final turn and held off the Norwegian's furious sprint to win the race for Italy by inches.

The thousands watching roared their acclaim for Silvio Fauner, for he had defeated the great Bjørn Dæhlie head-to-head. But Fauner placed the victory in the proper perspective:

"Since that race, many people have asked me, 'Who is your hero? Who was your inspiration in Lillehammer?' The answer is simple—for it is the same person. His name is Maurilio De Zolt."

GAETAN BOUCHER

It was perhaps fitting that Canada's 29-year-old Gaetan Boucher should skate in his last Olympic race before a home crowd at the 1988 Calgary Olympic Games. He was already a Canadian national hero, the finest speed skater the country had ever produced. With his whole nation watching, he would be attempting to defend the 1500-meter championship that he'd won four years before, in Sarajevo.

At 17, Boucher had begun his Olympic career at the 1976 Innsbruck Games, where he failed to win any medals. Four years later, in Lake Placid, the luck of the draw in the 1000-meter race paired him with America's Eric Heiden. Heiden would make Olympic history by winning five gold medals in five individual events.

"Heiden was the hero of the Games," said Boucher. "I had little chance to beat him. But I decided I would do my best and maybe something good would happen."

Something good did happen. Heiden defeated Boucher by 1 1/2 seconds, but their heat was so fast that Boucher ended up with a silver medal after all the pairs had raced.

With Heiden retiring after the 1980 Lake Placid Games, Boucher was given a good chance to stand on the top step of the awards podium in Sarajevo. Even before the Games began, he was given the honor of carrying the Canadian flag into the stadium during the Opening Ceremonies.

"People were saying that at the last two Olympics, the person who carried the flag on opening day didn't do very well," said Boucher with a smile. "But I had a lot of confidence in 1984, and I wanted to prove that carrying the flag doesn't mean you can't win."

Boucher finished third in the 500 meters and now had a bronze to go with his silver of four years before. Four days later in the 1000 meters, he was superb. He defeated his nearest competitor by almost a second to win the gold medal. He immediately called his parents.

"The first words he said to me on the phone were, 'I got you your gold medal,'" Cyrenus Boucher, Gaetan's father, said with a laugh. "We had a joke within the family. I told Gaetan that the first gold medal he won would be mine. The next one would be his."

Two days later, Gaetan Boucher made Canadian Olympic history by winning

the 1500 meters. He became the first Canadian Winter Olympian to win two gold medals. His total of four medals was also the largest number ever won by a Canadian athlete.

At 6:00 P.M. on February 20, 1988, at the Calgary speed skating oval, 29-year-old Boucher made final preparations for his start in the 1500 meters, his last race in a career that spanned four Olympic Games.

Forty of the fastest skaters in the world would compete in pairs—two men against each other and against the clock. For the first time in Olympic history, the speed skating championships would be held indoors. The new 400-meter Calgary oval was the fastest in the world, and records were expected to fall in nearly every event.

Boucher drew the 15th of 20 pairs. This fact had particular significance—all of the other favorites in the race drew earlier pairs. Boucher would know in advance how fast a time he would have to skate to win.

The strength of the opposition became clear when the very first pair skated, for Eric Flaim of the United States shattered the world record.

This new record lasted less than eight minutes. In the third pair, Andre Hoffmann of East Germany broke Flaim's record by $6/100$ of a second.

Hoffmann's world record time held up as pair after pair competed. Finally, it was time for the 15th pair—and for Gaetan Boucher's final Olympic appearance.

Boucher went after the world record from the start. After 300 meters, his time was fastest of all. Nearing the halfway mark, he was still in the lead, but he was struggling. The home crowd urged him on, but Boucher could not respond. He was slowing down considerably. As Boucher struggled valiantly in the last lap before the finish, his father shouted from the stands, "Go Gaetan!" As Gaetan moved toward the finish line, Cyrenus Boucher looked at the clock. He stopped cheering and slowly sat down, tears streaming down his face.

After he crossed the finish line, Gaetan Boucher slowly circled the track. His time placed him ninth, but the thousands of fans stood to give him an ovation usually reserved for the winner. They knew that Gaetan Boucher had done his best, honoring the age-old philosophy that has sent Olympians into the arena for centuries: "Ask not alone for victory. Ask for courage. For if you can endure, you bring honor to yourself. Even more, you bring honor to us all."

BONNIE BLAIR

At the 1988 Calgary Olympics, 23-year-old Bonnie Blair was one of 30 competitors entered in the women's 500-meter speed skating event. This would be her second attempt at winning a medal in this race. Four years earlier, in Sarajevo, she had finished eighth behind East Germany's gold and silver medal winners, Christa Rothenburger and Karin Kania.

Between Sarajevo and Calgary, Blair showed that she could challenge the East Germans, at one point even taking the world record away from Kania. But two months before the Calgary Games, Rothenburger broke Blair's record and immediately became the favorite to retain her 500-meter title.

"Going into the 1988 Olympics, the East Germans were the ones to beat," said an unfazed Blair. "I had been looking up to Christa Rothenburger and Karin Kania for a long time. And now, all of a sudden, I was skating at their level. Now that I was where they were, I had to stop being in awe of them."

Skating in the second pair, Rothenburger quickly showed she was the one to beat. She skated magnificently to a time of 39.12, breaking her own world record by almost one-third of a second.

Two pairs later, it was Bonnie Blair's turn. For her, the critical part of the race would be the start.

"I got to the first 100-meter mark and I heard the time over the loudspeaker," said Blair. "At that point, I was two-hundredths of a second ahead of Christa. This was a good sign because usually Christa is ahead of me at 100 meters. So I thought if the rest of the race went according to my plan, I had a good chance of beating her."

Blair's thoughts were correct. When she crossed the finish line, the scoreboard showed she was $2/100$ of a second faster than Rothenburger—the exact lead she had at the 100-meter mark. Though there were 11 pairs still left to skate, Blair knew the gold medal was hers, and with it, the world record.

Bonnie Blair's victory in the 500 meters was an inspiration to Yvonne van Gennip of the Netherlands, who was not in the 500 meters but would later win three gold medals in the 1500-, 3000-, and 5000-meter events.

"I, like everybody else, was so fearful of the East German skaters," said van Gennip. "But when Bonnie won the 500 meters, she showed us all that they were not invincible."

Four days later, Blair won a bronze in the 1000 meters, finishing behind Rothenburger.

The year after the Calgary Games, Blair's father, Charlie, died after a long bout with cancer, and for a time she lost her will to train. Her father was one of the original members of the Blair Bunch—family and friends who would travel at their own expense to Bonnie's major competitions. But a year before the 1992 Albertville Games, Blair's competitive spirit returned.

In Albertville, 45 members of the Blair Bunch, led by Bonnie's mother, Eleanor, were in the stands to cheer her on.

In the 500 meters, Bonnie won by $18/100$ of a second over Ye Quiaobo of China and became the first American woman to win gold medals at two different Winter Olympics.

Four days later, Blair won the 1000 meters, again defeating Ye Quiaobo, this time by $2/100$ of a second. The fact that the American's three gold medals were won by a total margin of $22/100$ of a second illustrates just how close a speed skating competition can be.

Two years later, at the Lillehammer Games, on Saturday afternoon, February 19, 1994, Bonnie Blair was one month short of her 30th birthday when she prepared for the start of the 500 meters. In the stands at the Viking Ship Arena in Lillehammer were some 60 members of the Blair Bunch. Dressed in gray sweatshirts and gold caps emblazoned with the words GO BONNIE GOLD, the Blair Bunch was there to help Bonnie create Olympic history.

If she won the 500 meters, she would become the first speed skater, male or female, to win three successive gold medals in the same event.

Skating in the third pair, Blair was again magnificent. Though there were 28 women still left to skate, Bonnie was certain of victory. Again, she was correct. She won by more than a third of a second.

Four days later, in the 1000 meters, Bonnie was again the class of the field. This time, the race was not even close. Bonnie had won her first four medals by margins measured in infinitesimal parts of a second—this time, she won by more than a full second.

On the awards podium, as the U.S. national anthem was played for Blair for the fifth time, she thought of the one person who was missing.

"I love the victory ceremony," said Blair. "For you finally have a few moments to reflect on what has happened. There, my thoughts turned to my father. Even though he was not sitting with the Blair Bunch, I knew he was having just as much fun in heaven."

PEGGY FLEMING

On February 15, 1961, one of the most tragic events in sports history occurred when the plane carrying the U.S. figure skating team crashed in Brussels while en route to the World Figure Skating Championships in Prague. All 73 passengers were killed, including 18 members of the U.S. team, along with their trainers and coaches.

Among the victims were Maribel Vinson Owen and her daughter, Laurence. Maribel Vinson Owen was a three-time Olympian who had won the bronze medal behind Henie's second victory at the 1932 Lake Placid Games, and many believed that Laurence Owen would win the gold medals that her mother had never won.

Also killed in the crash was Billy Kipp, the coach of 12-year-old Peggy Fleming, an upcoming prodigy. When she heard the news, Peggy was devastated. She vowed to honor his memory by dedicating her career to him. For her, this meant becoming world and Olympic champion. But the skating world knew that it would be many years before the Americans would again be contenders. Besides losing their skaters, the United States had lost most of their top coaches.

"Skating, particularly in America, has received an incalculable setback," said famed coach and double Olympic pairs champion Pierre Brunet at the time. "It will take at least 10 years for an American to again challenge for top honors."

By the time she was 15, Peggy Fleming was well on her way to disproving Brunet's dire predictions. In 1964, she became the youngest U.S. national champion, winning the first of five successive national championships. She went on to finish sixth in the 1964 Innsbruck Olympics. Just three years after the fatal plane crash, she had catapulted American skating back onto the international scene.

The rise of Peggy Fleming was a family affair. Her beloved father, Albert, knew that she had a special talent. After Innsbruck, he moved the family to Colorado Springs so that Peggy could be coached by the legendary Carlo Fassi of Italy, himself a two-time European champion. At the 1965 World Championships in Colorado Springs, Fleming won the bronze medal, skating in a costume made by her mother.

"I could not have accomplished anything without my family," she said. "Dad, Mom, and my sisters made so many sacrifices. My father would work double

shifts as a newspaper pressman so there would be money for me to train and travel."

A year after moving to Colorado, Fleming amazed the skating world when, at 17, she won her first world championship title in Davos, Switzerland. It was the first world title won by an American since Carol Heiss won the last of her five straight titles in 1960.

Fleming successfully defended her world title in 1967 in Vienna. Afterward, under coach Carlo Fassi, she began six-hour-a-day training sessions in preparation for her ultimate quest: to become the 1968 Olympic champion in Grenoble, France.

Fleming arrived in Grenoble a heavy favorite, already winning accolades from the greats of the sport, including Dick Button, America's double-gold medal winner in 1948 and 1952.

"She is an exquisite skater," said Button, "so lyrically expressive and technically perfect. With some skaters, there is a lot of fuss and feathers, but nothing is happening. With Peggy, there's no fuss and feathers, and a great deal is happening."

In Grenoble, Fleming built a large lead during the compulsory figures. Barring a catastrophe, the question was not whether she would win but rather by what margin of victory.

When she completed her free-skating performance, which included extravagant moves that no one could duplicate, one judge commented, "Peggy Fleming is the best figure skater to ever step onto the ice." The other judges confirmed that comment—all nine gave her first place votes.

There was one additional honor for Peggy Fleming. She was the only American gold medal winner at the 1968 Grenoble Games.

Phil (left) and Steve Mahre.

PHIL AND STEVE MAHRE

"Why was that guy given another chance?" a first-time spectator asked his friend after watching a skier finish his run down the slalom course.

The uninitiated have asked the same question countless times.

"That was Phil Mahre," laughed the friend. "The other guy you're talking about was his twin brother, Steve."

Phil and Steve Mahre, identical twins raised in a small town at the foot of Washington state's Cascade Mountains, remain one of the greatest brother acts in Olympic history.

As 18-year-olds at the 1976 Innsbruck Games, they competed at the Olympics for the first time. They didn't win any medals, but Phil finished a commendable fifth in the giant slalom.

Four years later, at the Lake Placid Games, Phil Mahre was the first starter in the slalom. To many, it was a minor miracle that he was still competing, for he had recovered from a severe injury in 1979 that required the insertion of a metal plate and four screws in his left ankle.

Three days earlier in the giant slalom, Phil had finished 10th and Steve 15th in a race won by the magnificent Ingemar Stenmark of Sweden.

Phil's first run in the slalom was excellent. His time held him in first place through the next 11 skiers, including his brother Steve, who missed a gate and was disqualified.

The 13th skier was Stenmark, going after his second gold medal in Lake Placid. To everyone's surprise, Stenmark's first run was more than half a second slower than Phil's, leaving him in fourth place.

For the second run, the top five skiers went off in reverse order. Phil Mahre, still in the lead after the first run, would be the last to start.

Stenmark was the fourth-to-last competitor. He turned in a spectacular run, taking over first place, with three skiers left.

"I knew my second run was a good one," said Stenmark. "But I was worried about Phil because he still had a good chance. I wish I had skied faster."

The next two skiers failed to overtake Stenmark. Phil Mahre was the only one left with a chance to win.

But Phil's run was a mediocre one—more than a second slower than Stenmark's. Still, it was good enough to win a silver medal behind the Swede.

"It's almost unexplainable how good Stenmark is," said Phil Mahre. "He's got such marvelous technique to go along with his amazing athletic ability. It's astounding how he always knows what he must do on the second run after he gets behind on the first."

Phil Mahre came away from the 1980 Games with some glory—he was the first American male alpine skier to win a medal in 16 years, and the first American to medal in the alpine events at the Lake Placid Games.

Four years later, the brothers were back again in the Olympic arena in Sarajevo.

This time, Stenmark would not be there to oppose them. He was prohibited from competing in the Games for being a "professional," a surprise, since most of the world's top skiers were known to have large bank accounts from sponsorships and endorsements.

Timing played a particularly large part in Phil's thoughts in Sarajevo. He wanted to win the slalom gold medal. But even more important, he was eager to get back home to be with his wife, Dolly, who was expecting their child, due a week after the slalom competition.

After the first run, Steve Mahre was in first place, almost $^{70}/_{100}$ of a second ahead of Jonas Nilsson of Sweden. Phil Mahre was in third, a few hundredths of a second behind Nilsson.

The second run would again go in reverse order, with Phil going down third from last, and Steve the final seeded skier to leave the starting line.

"When I got to the finish after my second run," said Phil, "I was celebrating. I knew I had at least won the bronze. Then, when Nilsson finished, I knew that I had the silver and only Steve had a chance to win the gold. I got on the walkie-talkie and basically told him everything he must do to beat me, which is probably something that doesn't happen in sports anymore—telling an opponent, even if he is in the family. If I couldn't win, he'd better win."

Unfortunately, Steve made several mistakes on his second run. Although he was the eighth fastest, his combined time was still good enough to win the silver medal behind Phil's gold.

History was made in Sarajevo—two brothers winning the gold and silver medals—reminiscent of the performance of the Goitschel sisters, Marielle and Christine, who took turns winning the gold and silver medals for France in the slalom and giant slalom 20 years before, at the 1964 Innsbruck Games.

On his way to the victory ceremony, Phil Mahre received the news that he did not have to rush home. Earlier that day, his wife had given birth to their son—one week before he was expected.

MYRIAM BÉDARD

Few people outside of the sport can name an Olympic biathlon gold medal winner. It is not a marquee attraction, but it is one of the most grueling yet precise events contested—a cross-country ski race interspersed with target shooting at designated intervals along the course. A biathlete must be an excellent cross-country skier, but proficiency with a rifle is even more critical, as large penalties are assessed for each missed target.

At the 1994 Lillehammer Games, two individual biathlon events were scheduled for women—the 15 kilometers and 7.5 kilometers. When these two events were completed, Olympic history had been made by a 24-year-old Canadian named Myriam Bédard.

Bédard was an unlikely candidate for the biathlon. Her first love was figure skating, and she dreamed of winning an Olympic gold medal, just as Canada's Barbara Ann Scott had in 1948. But figure skating is an expensive sport, and Bédard's family did not have the finances to support her.

"When I had to leave figure skating, I was attracted to the biathlon because of the solitude of the sport," said Bédard. "I love to ski the trails alone—it gives me a tranquil feeling. There is so much beauty in being alone."

Bédard was an immediate success in Canada. From 1987 to 1989, she was Canadian junior champion. In 1990, she won the Canadian senior championship. That same year, she sprung into international prominence by winning the silver medal in the 15 kilometers at a World Cup event in Austria, followed by an eighth place finish at the 1990 World Championships. In 1991, the year before the Albertville Games, she was ranked second in the World Cup standings.

Bédard's need to control her own destiny was never more evident than when she took on a European coach a few months before the 1992 Albertville Olympics, much to the chagrin of Canadian biathlon officials.

But her independence paid off when she won the bronze medal in the 15 kilometers, the first biathlon medal ever won by a Canadian.

The year following the Albertville Olympics, Bédard dominated the world championships, winning the gold in the 7.5 kilometers and the silver in the 15 kilometers.

Five days before she was to start in the 15 kilometers at the 1994 Lillehammer

Games, Bédard went into seclusion. She became a virtual hermit, speaking to no one and eating her meals away from the hubbub of the athletes' village.

In the 15 kilometers, her first event, there were four shooting stops at specific parts of the course. During the race, each skier would take a total of 20 shots: five prone, five standing, five prone, and finally, five standing.

The key to the biathlete's success is to ski fast, then know when to ease into the shooting stops, slowing down the heart rate in order to hold the rifle steady enough to hit the target. The penalty is severe for a missed shot—60 seconds added to the contestant's overall time for each miss.

On the morning of February 18, Bédard emerged from her seclusion for the 15 kilometers. She skied a marvelous race, but she was even more sensational in the shooting phase. Of the 20 attempts, she missed only two. Although she was given two penalty minutes, her closest competitors had both missed three targets. When the scores were tabulated, Myriam Bédard had won by more than 46 seconds. She became the first Canadian ever to win a biathlon gold medal.

Five days later, the 7.5 kilometers was scheduled. In this race, the biathlete is required to make two stops: five shots from the prone position a third of the way into the race, and five shots standing at the 5-kilometer mark.

The penalty for missing a target in the 7.5 kilometers differs from the 15 kilometers. Instead of a 60-second time penalty, a miss in the 7.5 kilometers requires the biathlete to ski a 150-meter penalty loop.

For most of the event, Bédard appeared to be on her way to an easy victory. At the first shooting stop, she hit all five targets in the prone position.

She continued her streak with her first three shots in the standing position. But then, disaster struck. Bédard missed her final two shots, forcing her to take two 150-meter penalty loops. With $2^1/_2$ kilometers left for her to ski, she was 16 seconds behind the leader.

"At first, I thought the task was impossible," she said. "But then I said to myself, 'You can't quit now,' so I just pressed on."

Those who were there witnessed one of the greatest finishes of the Lillehammer Games. With one kilometer left, she was still seven seconds behind. Bédard was relentless, sprinting the entire kilometer to the finish. When she crossed the finish line, she threw her arms up high as she watched the scoreboard flash the news. She had won her second gold medal, by a little more than a second.

Myriam Bédard had again made Canadian Olympic history. She became the first Canadian woman ever to win two gold medals in the same Winter Games.

YVONNE VAN GENNIP

As the 1988 Calgary Winter Games approached, it was predicted that the women speed skaters from East Germany would again dominate the competition. Four years earlier, they had won every gold and silver medal in the speed skating events at the Sarajevo Games.

But in Calgary, Bonnie Blair of the United States shocked the skating world when, in the 500 meters, she defeated the powerful East German Olympic champions—defending gold medalist Christa Rothenburger and her teammate, Karin Kania, who had won the 500 meters four years earlier, in Sarajevo. One of the spectators watching from the stands was Yvonne van Gennip of the Netherlands, who would later compete against the East Germans in the 1500-, 3000-, and 5000-meter races.

"Before that 500-meter race, all the skaters were fearful of the East Germans," recalled van Gennip. "But when Bonnie defeated them, I rushed over to her and congratulated her. I told her, 'You have given me a great deal of confidence... confidence that the East Germans can be beaten."

Many believe that van Gennip's appearance in Calgary was a miracle. Two months before the Games, she had undergone surgery on a badly infected right foot. Leaving the hospital after just two weeks of recuperation, she stepped onto the ice in her first practice not certain she would be ready. One month before the Games, just when she had announced that her recovery was complete, van Gennip suffered another setback. She learned that her personal coach, Tjaard Kloosterboer, would not be coming to Calgary.

"I had trained with Tjaard Kloosterboer for four years," she said. "But the Dutch Olympic Committee decided that the team should be under the guidance of our head coach, Egbert vant Oever. I was very sad that Tjaard was not in Calgary. So I did the next best thing. Every day I would telephone him two or three times for advice, and we would talk as if he were there with me."

In her first race in Calgary, the 3000 meters, van Gennip was up against three East German superstars. In the first pair, defending Olympic champion Andrea Ehrig destroyed the world record by almost five seconds.

By the time van Gennip stepped to the starting line in the fourth pair, it appeared that the East German women would again sweep the event. They already held the first-, second-, and third place positions.

Van Gennip skated a marvelous race, but with one lap to go, it seemed that the gold medal was out of reach. Though solidly ahead of the East Germans in second and third places, she was still almost a full second behind Ehrig's world record time.

"I heard the crowd screaming, so I knew I was doing well," recalled van Gennip. "So I said to myself, 'Perhaps there is a chance.' I just skated hard and fast, and as I crossed the finish line I heard the crowd giving a tremendous roar."

Van Gennip had turned in a time $^{15}/_{100}$ of a second faster than Ehrig's. The gold medal and world record were hers.

Four days later, in the 1500 meters, Yvonne van Gennip would again face the two East German champions, Andrea Ehrig and Karin Kania.

"Until the 3000-meter victory, the press people were always talking to the East Germans," van Gennip said. "Now they were talking a little bit more to me."

Kania and Ehrig were in first and second places as van Gennip got ready to skate.

"I watched Yvonne van Gennip's race," recalled Kania. "With the race half over, she was two-tenths of a second behind my time. But I was not confident. With two laps to go, I knew she was capable of making up the time...particularly since her last lap in the 3000 meters had been so fast."

Kania's fears were well-founded. In the final 800 meters, van Gennip was spectacular. She defeated Kania by $^{14}/_{100}$ of a second to win her second gold medal.

On Sunday afternoon, February 28, 1988, the 5000 meters was scheduled—the final skating event on the last day of the Olympic Games. Although van Gennip held the world record, it was the first time the distance would be contested in an Olympic competition.

Again skating in the first pair, Ehrig quickly wiped out van Gennip's record by more than three seconds. Ehrig's time held up for the next three pairs. Finally, in the fifth pair, van Gennip stepped to the starting line. Before the Games, it was predicted that this would be the only event that van Gennip could challenge for a gold medal.

"This was my strongest race," she said. "When Ehrig broke my world record, I was not too worried. I knew what I had to do."

With just a few hundred meters left in the race, van Gennip was almost three seconds faster than Ehrig. She maintained that margin to the finish line. Yvonne van Gennip had won her third gold medal.

After the Games, van Gennip returned to a hero's welcome in her hometown of Haarlem.

"I think everyone needs a goal in life," van Gennip told the cheering audience. "But that doesn't mean that the goal has to be the highest one. I feel that winning medals is not so important. Rather, it is important to be a person of high character."

ULRICH WEHLING

Ulrich Wehling is a hometown hero to the people of Oberwiesenthal, in eastern Germany. He is known there as one of the most versatile athletes ever to compete—having won championships in cycling, cross-country running, tennis, the high jump, and the shot put.

But Wehling has another distinction. Outside of Oberwiesenthal, he is perhaps the greatest unknown Olympic champion in the history of the Winter Games. Although he competed in three successive Olympics—1972, 1976, and 1980—his event, the nordic combined, is one of the least-known on the Olympic program.

The nordic combined is a two-day event that taxes the athlete in two contrasting disciplines: ski jumping on a 70-meter hill the first day, and cross-country skiing over a 15-kilometer course the next. The winner is decided by the highest combined total of points earned in each phase of the competition.

Wehling's natural athletic abilities were perfectly suited to the nordic combined. As a 19-year-old, he competed in his first Olympic nordic combined at the 1972 Games in Sapporo. He finished fourth in the ski jump and third in the cross-country ski race. His combined score won him the gold medal.

After the Sapporo Games, Wehling won almost every major championship he entered, making him the heavy favorite as the competition began at the 1976 Innsbruck Games.

"I was very fortunate in the ski jump," recalled Wehling. "I had two excellent jumps and was in first place by a wide margin going into the ski race. But the victory was not going to be as easy for me as everyone thought."

No one knew that Wehling's vision was seriously impaired.

"I had a severe eye infection and could see only out of one eye," he explained. "My vision in that eye was blurred, and it was difficult to distinguish the bumps, which slowed me down a bit. I finished the cross-country race in 13th place, but my margin of victory in the ski jump more than compensated for my poor showing. Fortunately, my combined total was just good enough to give me my second gold medal."

Afterward, Wehling thought about quitting international competition.

"I had accomplished my goals and I thought at the time I'd had enough," he said. "I had a serious knee operation, so I was asked to retire and start training

our younger athletes. Then my knee recovered completely, and I decided I wanted to try one more time."

At the 1980 Lake Placid Games, Wehling was again superb in the ski jump. He made the two longest jumps of his Olympic career to finish in first place, again giving him the lead at the start of the next day's 15-kilometer cross-country race.

Unlike in Innsbruck, this time Wehling began the second day facing serious challenges from two athletes: Finland's Jouko Karjalainen and Wehling's team-mate Konrad Winkler, who had won the bronze medal four years earlier when Wehling won his second gold. Both men were faster skiers than Wehling, and both had jumped well enough to be within striking distance of Wehling's lead.

In the nordic combined, the ski race is against the clock, with each of the finalists sent off in 20-second intervals. Fortunately for Wehling, he would start after Karjalainen and Winkler were on the course, allowing his coaches to give him advice along the route as to what he must do to win.

Both Karjalainen and Winkler finished with faster times than Wehling, but not by enough to overcome Wehling's superiority in the ski jump. Once again, Wehling's jumping had carried him to victory.

There was an additional accolade for Ulrich Wehling: He joined figure skaters Gillis Grafström and Sonja Henie to become only the third athlete to win three successive gold medals in the same event at the Winter Olympics.

JACK SHEA

At 10:00 A.M., February 4, 1932, thousands in the stands cheered as more than 300 athletes representing 17 countries marched in the Opening Ceremonies of the Lake Placid Winter Olympic Games.

The Games were formally opened by New York Governor Franklin Delano Roosevelt, who nine months later would be elected president of the United States.

Reciting the Olympic oath on behalf of all the athletes was 21-year-old speed skater Jack Shea, a native of Lake Placid.

"To be chosen to take the Olympic oath was a great honor in itself," said Shea. "It was an honor for me and my community."

Soon after reciting the oath, Shea stepped to the starting line for his heat in the 500 meters.

This would be Jack Shea's first confrontation with the renowned European speed skaters. But here in Lake Placid, Shea had an advantage. For the first time, the speed skating events would be run according to North American rules, which featured massed starts, with all skaters racing at once, as opposed to the European style of two-contestant heats racing against the clock.

Four years earlier, the 500-meter gold medal had been shared by Finland's Clas Thunberg and Norway's Bernt Evensen, both finishing in a time of 43.4 seconds.

Evensen came to Lake Placid to try again, but Thunberg was so incensed over having to skate under North American "pack racing" rules that he refused to enter the competition.

Six men made it to the final of the 500 meters, including Shea and Evensen. The four other finalists were either Canadian or American.

Shea took the lead immediately, and although Evensen pressed him down the stretch, the American won by five yards.

"I was taught early never to look back," he said. "Coming down the stretch, I could hear Evensen's skates. I wanted to look back, but fortunately I didn't. That could have been a fatal error."

The following day, the 1500-meter race was scheduled. Three Americans and three Canadians made it to the final. Jack Shea was one of them.

Coming off the final turn, Shea was in second place behind his teammate

Herbert Taylor. But as they came out of the turn, Taylor slipped and tumbled. Shea went on to win his second gold medal.

Records of Jack Shea's participation at the 1932 Olympics have a dramatic significance. At the Opening Ceremonies, Shea recited the Olympic oath from the second step of the awards podium, the spot designated for the silver medal winner. Ironically, before two nightfalls would pass, Shea would twice stand on the same podium—but on the top step, as the winner of two Olympic gold medals.

"When I was a child, I'd always dreamed I would win something that would cause the American flag to be raised in my honor while 'The Star Spangled Banner' played," said Shea more than four decades later. "I'm prouder of it today than I was in 1932."

MANUELA DI CENTA AND LYUBOV EGOROVA

As the 1994 Lillehammer Games approached, 27-year-old Lyubov Egorova of Russia was little known outside her sport of cross-country skiing. Yet she was coming to the Games with one of the best records in Winter Olympic history.

Two years earlier, at the Albertville Games, Egorova competed in all five women's events as a member of the Unified Team, made up of former Soviet athletes. When the Albertville Games were over, Egorova had won three gold and two silver medals—the greatest individual medalist of the Games.

She would compete in the same five events at the Lillehammer Olympics. One of those opposing her would be Manuela Di Centa of Italy. This would be Di Centa's fourth Olympics. In her three previous appearances, she'd won a single medal—a bronze as part of the Italian relay team at the 1992 Albertville Games.

On February 13, 1994, one day after the Opening Ceremonies, the women's 15 kilometers was scheduled. Fifty-four women would race against the clock, starting off at 30-second intervals. The 44th skier out was Manuela Di Centa. Egorova would be 47th, 90 seconds after Di Centa.

"The 15 kilometers was very special to me, for it was in that event that I won my first gold medal two years before, in Albertville," Egorova recalled. "It was not only my first but the first gold medal awarded at the Games."

Di Centa started swiftly and skied a superb race. At the finish, Di Centa defeated Egorova by more than a minute, and the Russian champion had to settle for the silver medal. But Egorova's medal streak was still intact. In six races, spanning two Olympics, she had won three gold and three silver medals.

Two days later, Egorova got her revenge in the 5-kilometer race, finishing 20 seconds ahead of Di Centa to win the gold medal. Equally important, the 5 kilometers counted as the first leg of the two-day combined pursuit event, meaning that two days later, Egorova would get a 20-second head start on Di Centa in the second leg: 10 kilometers, skied head-to-head, with the first one across the finish line winning the gold medal for the combined.

"It was extremely difficult to defeat Egorova when we started even," Di Centa said. "To defeat her with a 20-second handicap would be next to impossible."

Di Centa was correct. Although she skied a faster 10 kilometers than Egorova,

Manuela Di Centa (center) celebrating her gold medal in the 1994 15K, flanked by two Russians—silver medalist Lyubov Egorova (left) and bronze medalist Nina Gavriluk. It was the first of four times that Di Centa and Egorova would share the podium in Lillehammer.

she could only make up 12 seconds of the 20-second deficit. At the finish, Egorova was in front by almost 40 meters.

With two events left, Egorova and Di Centa were now battling for individual honor. In the three events completed, Egorova had won two gold medals and one silver, and Di Centa one gold and two silver.

On Monday, February 21, came the women's 4 x 5-kilometer relay. Of the 14 countries entered, Russia was the favorite, with Norway and Italy expected to be the only serious challengers.

The race was close throughout the first three legs, but Egorova, skiing the anchor position for the Russians, was sensational. Although she started her leg in second place, she crossed the finish line 30 seconds ahead of the field. Norway was second, followed by Italy.

After four events, Egorova had won three gold medals and one silver. As part of the third place Italian relay team, Di Centa, too, had medaled in all four events—one gold, two silver, and one bronze.

On Thursday, February 24, 53 women were scheduled to start in the 30-kilometer race, the longest and most grueling event on the women's program.

Egorova was on the verge of making Olympic history. If she won the 30 kilometers, it would be her seventh gold medal—more than any athlete in Winter Olympic history. Winning any medal would tie her with her friend and idol Raisa Smetanina, who'd won 10 medals in five Olympics.

Once the 30-kilometer event was under way, it was immediately apparent that Egorova was not the same skier she had been in her previous races. At the halfway mark, she was in seventh place, more than a minute behind the leader—Manuela Di Centa.

"I was very tired for this race," Egorova said. "That is why this sport is so uncertain. Your performance can change from day to day. Two years ago, in Albertville, I was four minutes faster than Di Centa. Now in Lillehammer she was a minute faster than me."

Di Centa continued to ski magnificently, going on to win the gold medal. Egorova tried valiantly, but the best she could do was fifth, the first time in two Olympics that she had failed to win a medal. When it was over, Di Centa had done what Egorova could not—she won a medal in all five events.

That night, the victory ceremony took place.

"I was happy but also a little sad," said Di Centa. "I was happy winning two gold, two silver, and a bronze medal. But standing on the awards podium, there was something missing. For the first time in five victory celebrations in Lillehammer, Lyubov Egorova and I would not be standing beside each other."

BILL JOHNSON

Before a fight, Muhammed Ali raised eyebrows among members of the press by reciting a poem that would name the round in which his opponent would fall. He was often right, much to the chagrin of his detractors.

"It ain't braggin' if he does it," wrote one columnist, and subsequent Ali poems were treated with greater respect.

Bill Johnson of the United States brought back memories of Ali when he arrived in Sarajevo to compete in the downhill at the 1984 Winter Olympic Games.

Brash, cocky, and outspoken, the 23-year-old Johnson gained few friends among his opponents and the world press. He told them that the race was a formality—the victory was already his, and the contest was for the silver and bronze medals.

Johnson had always caused as much controversy with his lifestyle as he did with his words. He'd been arrested for stealing a car when he was a few months shy of his 18th birthday, and prosecutors wanted to try him as an adult.

"That really scared the devil out of me," Johnson remembered. "But they finally decided it was a juvenile court case. Thank goodness the judge just gave me a reprimand and warned that the next time I would not be so lucky."

When he was 19, Johnson received a scholarship to the Alpine Training Center in Lake Placid and later was named to the U.S. national team.

Although he appeared at the 1980 Lake Placid Games and practiced with the team, his participation was limited to being a forerunner—one of the skiers who tests the course before the actual competition begins.

The following year, Johnson was tossed off the team during summer training. He refused to go through the dry-land drills. In addition, Johnson appeared to be out of shape and couldn't pass the running and weight room minimums.

"I had just recovered from the flu, and the ski competitions were still six months away," said Johnson. "I would have been in great shape if I hadn't been tossed out."

Getting thrown off the team turned out to be one of the best things that ever happened to Johnson, and the key to his performance in Sarajevo. His exile forced him to train on the U.S. domestic circuit for a year, where he perfected his aerodynamic tuck on the flatter American courses. He also got himself into great shape so he could get back on the team. By the time he was allowed back in 1982, he had the best tuck of anyone on the team in wind tunnel tests. But in the years leading to Sarajevo, Johnson continued to be the cause of much concern to his teammates and coaches. His arrogance annoyed everyone on a daily basis.

After a mediocre 1983–1984 season, Johnson's mouth was still bigger than his downhill results. But on January 15, 1984, one month before the Olympic final, he turned in a spectacular downhill victory in the famed Lauberhorn in Wengen, Switzerland.

During the five practice runs before the actual race in Sarajevo, Johnson's performances began to match his press conference predictions. He ended up with two firsts, two seconds, and a fourth, by far the best practice record of any of the downhillers. Some members of the press were now taking Johnson's pronouncements more seriously.

"This course was made for me," he said with certainty. "If I'm among the leaders after the twisting turns of the top half of the course, nothing can stop me. On the lower half, the flatland, there is no one in the world that can stay with me."

Olympic history gave little credence to Johnson's words. Since the downhill's introduction in 1948, the gold medal had always been won by French, Italian, Austrian, and Swiss skiers. No American male had ever stood on the top step of the awards podium in any alpine event. In the downhill, the highest American finish was fifth.

Johnson was the sixth of 61 skiers to go off.

His time at the halfway point put him in fourth place, a little more than half a second behind the leader. Once he was tight in his tuck, Johnson was the best glider in the race—if he made no mistakes on the flatter lower half, the gold medal would be his.

He finished the race, declaring himself the winner. Though there were still 55 skiers to go, he was correct. His time of 1:45.59 held up through the entire competition. In second and third places were skiers from the countries that sent the perennial gold medal winners—Peter Mueller of Switzerland, 27/100 of a second behind, and Anton Steiner of Austria, 36/100 of a second behind.

In his moment of victory, Johnson was as ungracious as ever.

"I'm glad it was the Swiss and Austrians for the silver and bronze," he said, smiling broadly. "They always think they've got the race locked. I wanted to stick it to them."

DOROTHY HAMILL

A columnist once called Dorothy Hamill "beautiful and majestic." The columnist was only partly right, for the engaging smile and balletlike moves of the 5-foot 3-inch Hamill were a theatrical facade. Inside was a frightened, taut, unconfident performer who often wished she were somewhere else. Such was the contradiction that was played out every time Hamill stepped onto the ice for a major—or even a minor—championship.

"It's like going to an execution," Hamill often said. "Standing in the dressing room before I go on, there are no positive thoughts. Am I going to fall? Why am I doing this?"

She grew up in Riverside, Connecticut, and skated for the first time when she was 9, wearing a pair of store-bought skates that cost a mere $5.95. Her love for the ice was immediate, and her parents were behind her from the start, both emotionally and financially.

"My folks said, 'If you want to skate, that's fine,'" Hamill recalled. "But they gave me one bit of stern advice. 'We're with you...as long as you work hard.'"

Hamill did work hard, practicing seven hours a day, six days a week.

In 1973, the Hamills moved to Denver, mainly so that Dorothy could be coached by the famed Italian Carlo Fassi. It was eight years earlier that Peggy Fleming's family had made the same decision. The move was a fortuitous one for Fleming, for under Fassi's guidance she won the 1968 Olympic figure skating gold medal in Grenoble.

Fassi's teaching also had great results for Hamill. She won successive U.S. National Championships and represented the United States at the 1975 World Championships. There Hamill suffered the first major setback of her career—coming in second to Dianne de Leeuw of the Netherlands. Nevertheless, she was improving and was still given a good chance to defeat de Leeuw the following year at the 1976 Innsbruck Games.

Hamill came to Innsbruck without the fanfare that greeted Peggy Fleming eight years earlier in Grenoble. But the comparisons were inevitable.

"They are quite different," said Carlo Fassi. "Dorothy is better on spins and is more powerful and athletic. Peggy is more of the ballet school."

As the Innsbruck Games approached, panic set in for Hamill, which she dramatically described in her book *On and Off the Ice*.

"I won my third U.S. National Championship in January, a month before the Games," Hamill wrote. "But I was unhappy with my performance. One of the problems was my relationship with Carlo Fassi. I got the feeling he was paying little attention to me. After the nationals, Carlo left to supervise John Curry for the European Championships. I was very upset. My mother then asked Peter Burrows, a coach living in New York, to work with me at his Skyrink Club.... Peter pulled my head together and motivated me. Peter had been so helpful that my mother asked the U.S. Figure Skating Association if he could come to Innsbruck as my coach. But they refused to give Peter permission."

The figure skating competition at the 1976 Games was different from today's version. Then, the competition was divided into three separate disciplines—compulsories counting for 30 percent of the final score; a two-minute short program counting for 20 percent; and finally the four-minute freestyle program, worth 50 percent.

If Hamill was nervous as she stepped onto the ice for the compulsory figures, she did not show it. When the last skater had finished, she was in second place.

She was even more spectacular in the two-minute short program, moving into first place. This was a reversal of what took place at the world championships a year before, when de Leeuw was in front leading up to the four-minute free-skating final.

Hamill was the picture of calm, the 14th skater of the final evening's free-skating program. But again, this masked her true feelings.

"I was standing in the center of the ice," she wrote in her autobiography, "trying to still the thudding of my heart. My knees were trembling slightly. I felt enormous pressure as I waited what seemed like hours for my music to start. Finally, I thought of Carlo Fassi's words. 'Focus your mind into a tunnel and look to the other end where the light is shining.'"

The light did shine for Dorothy Hamill. She turned in a nearly error-free skating routine. Combining caution with an occasional flair for the spectacular, she protected her lead, receiving 5.8s and 5.9s out of a possible 6 for both technical and artistic merit. Even more important, when the tabulations were in, Hamill was named the winner by all nine judges.

For Fassi, it was a historic Olympic Games. His other pupil, John Curry of Great Britain, also won the gold medal—the first time that one coach had two pupils on the top step of the awards podium in the same Olympics.

TOMAS GUSTAFSON

When he was not competing, speed skater Tomas Gustafson of Sweden spent most of his time in solitude, writing poetry in the woods near his hometown of Eskiltuna. While Gustafson is a national hero in Sweden, compared with the publicity received by America's Bonnie Blair and Eric Heiden, Gustafson is little known outside of his sport. Nevertheless, he is one of the greatest champions in Winter Olympic history.

On the afternoon of February 17, 1988, Gustafson stepped to the starting line in the ninth pair of the 5000-meter event. Four years earlier, in Sarajevo, he had won this event and gone on to win the silver medal in the 10,000 meters. But for Gustafson, the four-year road to Calgary had been long and painful.

"After my successes in Sarajevo, my life was perfect—for a while," Gustafson recalled. "But following the Olympics, I had setback after setback, both on and off the ice. I totally missed out in the world championships. Then I suffered an attack of meningitis and could not train. I told my sponsor that he did not have to pay me. Then the worst thing of all happened. My father became very sick and died."

For a time, Gustafson's depression was so deep that he gave up all hope of competing in the Olympics again. But it was his trips to the woods, communing with nature, that gradually rejuvenated him.

"I just felt that inside there was still something I had to bring out," Gustafson recalled. "Slowly, I got the old motivation again, and I thought, 'I'm going to try again in Calgary.'"

Yet once in Calgary preparing for the start of his 5000-meter race, his thoughts were elsewhere.

"I came out on the ice 10 minutes before my race," Gustafson said. "I wasn't thinking about the competition. Rather, I thought about running in the woods."

Eight pairs would skate before him. From watching the earlier competitors, he already knew he would have to break the world record to win. The 5000 meters is $12\frac{1}{2}$ laps around a 400-meter oval. With one lap to go, Gustafson was still almost a second behind the leader, Leo Visser of the Netherlands. Gustafson's task seemed impossible.

But with the crowd roaring him on, he turned in a spectacular last lap. He defeated Visser by $35/100$ of a second.

Four days later, his confidence restored, Gustafson again drew a favorable pairing in the 10,000 meters, the race in which he had won the silver medal four years before. Once again he was in the ninth pair, and his major adversaries had already skated.

This time Gustafson let it be known early that he was the best in the world.

As he finished the next-to-last lap of the 25-lap race, Gustafson was more than seven seconds ahead of the leader, Michael Hadschieff of Austria. Only a fall would prevent Gustafson from reaching his goal.

With the crowd again roaring, he crossed the finish line to break the world record by $31/100$ of a second.

On the awards podium, Tomas Gustafson had many thoughts.

"My whole life flashed before me," he said. "I thought of my dad and how proud he would have been. And then I thought of how difficult the road had been...the many setbacks. And in those few minutes, hearing the anthem and seeing the Swedish flag being raised, I thought that this was such a special moment. I can only say, it was beautiful."

BRIAN BOITANO
AND BRIAN ORSER

Close friends and rivals Brian Boitano of the United States and Brian Orser of Canada had grim looks on their faces as they threw punches at each other backstage before the final night of the men's figure skating championship at the 1988 Calgary Olympic Games.

Crowds gathered and journalists rushed to the scene to witness the unthinkable—the Battle of the Brians that was supposed to take place on the ice later was actually being resolved with fists.

But something was wrong. None of the punches landed. After a few moments, the skaters stopped swinging, burst into laughter, and embraced. The crowd relaxed, and the journalists realized they were victims of a hoax. The two Brians were still friends, and this was their way of stopping all the Battle of the Brians hype.

In 10 previous meetings over the past 10 years, Orser had won seven times and Boitano three. But past performances lost their meaning on the evening of February 20, 1988, as more than 19,000 spectators packed the Saddledome in Calgary to witness the final phase of the three-day competition.

Though Boitano led Orser by $2/10$ of a point after the compulsory and short programs, everyone knew that the gold medal was up for grabs. For the first two disciplines counted for only 50 percent of the total score, and the final 50 percent would be awarded on this final night, when they would each skate a $4^1/2$-minute program that would decide the championship.

Orser had two important emotional factors going for him: Earlier, he had been given the honor of carrying the Canadian flag in the Opening Ceremonies, and tonight he would be performing before a home-country crowd that adored him.

As is the custom with elite skaters, those vying for the medals would skate in the last group of six. Boitano would be the 19th skater of the evening. Orser would be 21st.

The wait was taxing everyone. Though Boitano and Orser were close friends, they became distant backstage. Each prepared himself emotionally in his own way.

"I cried three times waiting to go on," Boitano said. "People wanted to know why I was hiding in a corner backstage. I didn't want them to see me crying."

Brian Boitano

Finally the time arrived for Brian Boitano to take the ice. "I didn't watch Brian's program," said Orser. "The blinders came on, and I was totally focusing on what I had to do."

As Boitano got into his program, his coach, Linda Leaver, watched from the sideline. "When he landed his first jump, I knew that this was going to be a good night," Leaver remembered. "Then he landed his second jump, and I knew it was going to be one of those special nights when he had what I call his 'magic feet.'"

Boitano's long program was magnificent, with only a few minor errors. But there was still an opening for Orser to win.

As Orser began his program, one of his first moves was a triple flip.

"I made a slight mistake," Orser said. "It probably wasn't noticed by the spectators. It wasn't a very obvious error and didn't disrupt my continuity."

"I couldn't watch Brian skate," said Boitano. "I went to the dressing room and locked myself in one of the bathroom stalls. I kept hearing the crowd yell and kept looking at my watch. When I saw that five minutes was up, I knew he had finished. I got up and as I left the dressing room I heard his last mark on the loudspeaker. It was a 6...a perfect 6. I was already preparing myself for the silver medal."

The final tabulation was nearly impossible to comprehend. Of the nine judges, four gave Orser their first place votes. Three of the judges voted for Boitano. The remaining two judges called Orser and Boitano even. The judges had ruled that ties would be broken by the skater with the highest score for technical merit. Both judges who called it a tie had given the technical merit category to Boitano. Brian Boitano was the Olympic champion by a 5–4 vote.

"When the result was final," said Boitano, "our eyes met. I looked at Brian, who seemed in a daze. He ran his hands from his head slowly down to his chin. I felt so badly even in victory. I looked him square in the face and said, 'What can I say?'"

Brian Orser

THE MIRACLE ON ICE

Before the 1980 Lake Placid Olympics took place, the consensus among experts was that the U.S. hockey team would finish no better than seventh in the 12-team tournament.

"I felt we were better than our seventh place seed," said American coach Herb Brooks. "I thought we had a chance of going as high as fourth."

The 12 teams were divided into two divisions—Red and Blue. The Soviet Union, the winner of five of the last six Olympic hockey gold medals, was the odds-on favorite to win the Red Division, followed by Finland or Canada.

The United States, in the Blue Division, was not likely to get past the qualifying round but instead was expected to lose at least three games to the powerful squads from Sweden, Czechoslovakia, and West Germany.

The U.S. team's first match was against Sweden. Trailing 1–0, the Americans scored with 27 seconds left in the game to tie the Swedes. This miraculous finish set the pattern for what was to come.

They would next face Czechoslovakia, the powerhouse of the Blue Division and the only team in the tournament believed to have a chance of defeating the Soviet Union in the final. The Czechs showed their superiority by easily defeating Norway in the first round 11–0.

But the Americans took no heed of the Czech strength. The young U.S. team defeated Czechoslovakia 7–3. Suddenly no one was laughing at Coach Brooks' pre-Olympic opinions.

Incredibly, the U.S. team then went on to easily defeat Norway, Romania, and West Germany. The United States and Sweden, with identical records of four victories and one tie, became the Blue Division's representatives in the championship round. Representing the Red Division were the teams from the Soviet Union and Finland.

The United States had gone five games without a defeat, but most predicted that the honeymoon was about to end. They were scheduled to face the Soviet Union in the first game of the medal round.

"The Soviets had thoroughly demolished us 10–3 in an exhibition game a few days before the Olympics," Brooks said. "They were fantastic and deserved their ranking. There were many of us who believed the Soviets were good enough to win the Stanley Cup."

The Americans would not be embarrassed again. They played the Soviets almost evenly for more than two periods, trailing 3–2. Then, nearly halfway through the third period, Mark Johnson scored for the Americans to tie the game.

Cries of "USA...USA...USA" resounded throughout the stadium, and American flags were flying everywhere. The atmosphere was euphoric, the crowd ready to explode.

One minute and 21 seconds later, the American captain, Mike Eruzione, took a pass from teammate Mark Pavelich and sent a 25-footer whistling past Soviet goaltender Vladimir Myshkin.

To most who were there and to the millions who watched on television, the rest of the game was a blur. Down 4–3, the Soviets went into a frenzy. It seemed that they had twice as many men on the ice as they buzzed the American cage with shot after shot, only to be turned back time and time again by the American goaltender, the spectacular Jim Craig.

Finally, the minutes ticked away to the final seconds, and the crowd counted off the last moments of the greatest upset in Olympic hockey history.

After the game, Lake Placid's Main Street became a mini-version of the celebration in New York City's Times Square on V-J Day at the end of World War II.

In a light snow, thousands of spectators, mostly Americans, walked up and down Main Street laughing and crying, embracing people they did not know— forgetting for a few minutes that the United States still had to win its final game against Finland to win the gold medal.

With the Cold War still on, the American victory over the Soviets was as political as it was athletic, as hundreds spontaneously joined in singing choruses of "The Star Spangled Banner" and "God Bless America." To many, the victory soothed the earlier news of President Carter's dramatic announcement that the United States would boycott the 1980 Moscow Summer Olympics to protest the Soviet Union's invasion of Afghanistan.

The final game for the gold medal was almost anticlimactic. Although the United States trailed Finland 2–1 at the end of the second period, most now believed that the question was not *whether* the Americans would win but *how* they would win.

Completely outplaying the Finns in the third period, the Americans scored three goals, while holding the Finns scoreless. When the final buzzer sounded with the Americans in front 4–2, what had seemed so impossible became a part of history. The young U.S. team's victory over the Soviets and its incredible journey to the top step of the awards podium would forever be remembered as the Miracle on Ice.

KATERINA WITT AND DEBI THOMAS

Although she finished last as an 11-year-old at the 1924 Olympic Games in Chamonix, Sonja Henie of Norway went on to the most successful career in figure skating history, winning three successive gold medals and 10 successive world championships.

As the 1988 Calgary Olympics approached more than a half-century later, 10 women had won Olympic gold medals, but not one had been able to win it twice. In Calgary, Katerina Witt of East Germany, the defending champion from the 1984 Sarajevo Games, was given a good chance to repeat.

Her opposition was expected to come from Debi Thomas of the United States, a pre-med student at Stanford University. Thomas was the only person who had defeated Witt in five years. After the first two disciplines, the compulsories and the short program, Thomas led Witt by 2/10 of a point. Backstage, the sharp difference in the personalities of Witt and Thomas was apparent as they waited to go on the ice for the final stage—the long program.

Witt appeared relaxed and at ease, smiling and flirting with photographers and officials. But the normally talkative and gregarious Debi Thomas spent much of her time backstage alone. She knew that Witt could be beaten. Two years earlier, she had defeated Witt for the world championship title, when the German had been the heavy favorite.

Witt was in a position to put great pressure on Thomas, for she would perform her program before the American. Thomas would be the evening's last skater.

Witt was trailing Thomas going into the long program. Skating to the music of Bizet's *Carmen*, she elected to play it safe and complete her program without making too many mistakes. The judges were not impressed, nor were the spectators—leaving reason to believe that if Thomas was at her best, she could win the gold medal.

Witt was followed by the perky and attractive Elizabeth Manley of Canada, who was in third place. Skating before the home crowd, Manley went all out with a series of jumps and spins that brought forth tremendous cheers.

Although her performance was the best of the evening, receiving seven first place votes from the nine judges, she was too far behind to make up for her mediocre marks in the compulsory and short-form disciplines.

Thomas was noticeably nervous. It certainly did not help when the last words

Katerina Witt in her final Olympic performance, Lillehammer, 1994.

from her coach before she began her program were, "You've got to be perfect to win." Thomas stepped onto the ice without responding to his words.

Thomas was anything but perfect. Like Witt before her, she chose to skate to the music of *Carmen*. Twenty seconds into her routine, she landed badly on her second jump. The mishap was emotionally demoralizing for the American champion and, from there on, she performed as if she knew her chances for victory had ended.

She missed two more triples, but finished with a flourish. The crowd responded politely, but they were still remembering the scintillating performance of their own Elizabeth Manley. When the scores were flashed, Manley moved to second place, sending Thomas to third.

Katerina Witt's strategy had worked. Rather than try to win the competition outright, she decided to place the burden on Thomas to lose. Witt became the first figure skater since Sonja Henie to win the gold medal more than once.

Debi Thomas, even in defeat, also made history. She became the first African-American athlete to stand on the awards podium at the Winter Olympic Games.

Turning professional after the Calgary Games, Witt could not compete in the 1992 Albertville Olympics, but she and many other skaters had their eligibility restored after a 1992 rule change by the International Skating Union. In 1994 in Lillehammer, Witt decided to try again. Her appearance was one of the most dramatic and poignant moments of the Games.

When Witt stepped onto the ice as the last skater in the long program, the thousands in the stands roared their acclaim, a tribute to her final Olympic performance. As she waited for her music to begin, she knew that the battle for the medals had already been decided, with the gold, silver, and bronze won by Oksana Baiul of Ukraine, Nancy Kerrigan of the United States, and Chen Lu of China, respectively.

The best that Witt could hope for was sixth or seventh place. But this time, she was competing not for medals but to pay homage to the brave people of Sarajevo, devastated by war. It was in Sarajevo, 10 years earlier, that Witt had won her first Olympic gold medal, in an arena that was now reduced to rubble.

As she moved majestically through her performance, she was the Katerina Witt of old—a skater of beauty and grace. As she executed her jumps and spins, the music turned solemn, almost prayerlike. The crowd quieted as the strains of "Where Have All the Flowers Gone?" flowed through the arena—in tribute to the city in which Witt had gained international fame as an Olympic champion.

When she finished her routine, the audience roared their approval. Although she would finish seventh, to them she was still the queen of the figure skating world.

"Why did I come to Lillehammer?" Witt remarked afterward. "I came because I wanted to share the Olympic experience just one more time."

DAN JANSEN

In the early afternoon of Friday, February 18, 1994, 28-year-old Dan Jansen of the United States was warming up on the 400-meter oval at Hamar, the scene of the speed skating competitions at the Lillehammer Olympic Games.

Jansen would skate in the fourth pair of the 1000 meters, the last race of his Olympic career, one that had begun 10 years earlier at the 1984 Sarajevo Games. Jansen was a reluctant participant, for the 1000 meters was not his favorite event. More importantly, he was still depressed over his performance four days earlier, when a slight slip rounding a turn cost him his chance at winning the gold medal in his favorite event, the 500 meters—a race he'd been unanimously expected to win.

Jansen finished eighth in the 500 meters, a continuation of a star-crossed career that earned him every reward but an Olympic gold medal—or for that matter, any Olympic medal. Now as he prepared for the 1000 meters, it was with the knowledge that he had stepped to the starting line seven times before but had never stood on the awards podium.

Ironically, it was in his first Olympic race as an 18-year-old at the 1984 Sarajevo Games that he'd had one of his best finishes—fourth place in the 500 meters. But the response he received from the press and the public when he missed a medal by $^{16}/_{100}$ of a second was not what he expected.

"Making the United States team for the Sarajevo Games was a dream come true," said Jansen. "I was extremely happy with my fourth place finish. But when I got home, all I read in the press reports was 'Too bad, no medal,' or 'Jansen fails to win a medal.' That's when I first realized that if you don't win a medal, you're nothing."

Four years later, Jansen was a favorite to win both the 500 and 1000 at the Calgary Games. But the competitions were secondary. During his stay in Calgary, he was constantly on the phone to home, where his beloved older sister Jane was losing a yearlong battle with leukemia.

"On the morning of my 500-meter race, I was woken up at 6:00 A.M. by my mom, who told me that Jane's blood pressure was dropping rapidly, that she wouldn't make it through the day," Jansen remembered sadly. "Jane couldn't talk, but Mom told me she nodded when I told her I would win the race for her."

Jane died three hours before he would step to the starting line in the second pair of the 500 meters.

Blocking out the tragedy, Jansen started well. But in the first turn, without warning, he went sprawling to the ice. To this day, he cannot explain what happened.

Four days later, he was entered in the 1000, and for three-quarters of the race he was the fastest of all the previous competitors. Skating down the backstretch on the final lap, Jansen went down again.

In two races, Jansen had failed to reach the finish line.

Four years later in Albertville, 26-year-old Jansen again entered the 500 and 1000 meters. One of the favorites to win, he finished fourth in the 500 meters. Clearly distraught, Jansen skated a lackluster 1000 meters and finished 26th out of 46 starters.

"Many times I thought about quitting," Jansen said. "But if you're considered to be one of the best in the world, finishing 26th in your last Olympic appearance is not the way you want to leave the arena."

In the two years leading to the 1994 Lillehammer Games, Jansen was practically unbeatable. He held the world record for the 500 meters and was the only skater at that time to go the distance in less than 36 seconds—a feat compared to Roger Bannister's breaking of the four-minute mile barrier on the track.

"I was so sure that Lillehammer would make up for all that happened in the past," Jansen said. "Coming to Lillehammer I had lowered my world records, and I easily won both 500-meter events at the world championships. I was winning 500-meter races by almost half a second, and that's a considerable distance in the 500."

Ironically, the 500-meter race in Lillehammer was scheduled six years to the day after his sister had died. As he had in Calgary, Jansen dedicated this race to her.

"Before the race, Dan was fine," remembered Peter Mueller, Jansen's coach, himself a gold medal winner in the 1000 meters at the 1976 Innsbruck Games. "He was a little nervous but not any more than any other race he's been in. He looked in great shape and ready to show what he could do."

Jansen would skate in the second pair out of the 20 entered. The skaters are actually racing against the clock, and the winner is the skater with the fastest time.

From the start, Jansen was flying. Then, without warning, on the final turn his left skate slipped slightly. An ominous spray of ice flew from his skate. In speed skating, this spray means the loss of infinitesimal parts of a second. He tried to make up for the mistake by going all out down the stretch.

But it was too late. Although only two pairs had raced, Jansen was 14/100 of a second behind the winner in the first pair. Before the afternoon was over, seven racers were faster. Jansen finished in eighth place.

Immediately after the competition, Jansen met with Mueller.

"I told him I was finished," said Jansen, remembering the meeting. "I told Peter that the 500 meters was my race, and I didn't even want to think about the 1000. I just wanted to go home. And Peter, calm as always, said 'I know how you feel. Let's think about it. We've still got four days till the 1000 meters.'"

Four days later, Jansen had recovered from his depression enough to enter the 1000 meters. It would be the last race of his Olympic career. Jansen had been working with a sports psychologist, Dr. Jim Loehr, to prepare him for the 1000 meters.

"I'd worked with Dr. Loehr since a year before the 1992 Albertville Games. I'd always feared the 1000 meters because I would always tire near the end. I would be doing fine till the last lap, and then the tiredness I feared would become a reality," Jansen said. "Then, at Dr. Loehr's suggestion, I started doing all these crazy things. I would write down 'I love the 1000 meters. I love the 1000 meters' on pieces of paper and tape them up in the bathroom and all around the house. When Dr. Loehr first told me to do this, I thought he needed more help than I did."

Jansen skated in the fourth pair of the 1000 meters. His start was perfect.

At 200 meters, Jansen's time was the second fastest of all the skaters in the three previous pairs.

"I wasn't thinking about a gold medal," Jansen recalled. "All I wanted to do was skate a good race and be standing when I got to the finish line. I wanted the Olympic saga to end so that there would be no more stories about me not being able to make it to the finish line standing up."

At 600 meters, Jansen's time was faster than all the previous skaters. This became particularly significant, since seven of the racers he would have to beat had personal-best times that were faster than Jansen's best time in this event.

As he came into the final turn, a small spray of ice flew from his left skate, but he did not lose his stride. Coming down the homestretch, he knew there was no tomorrow. As he crossed the finish line, he turned to the scoreboard with a look of indecision. Then, simultaneously, the crowd roared and Jansen's arms stretched into the air, a magnificent smile enveloping his face. He had broken Canadian Kevin Scott's world record by $^{11}/_{100}$ of a second.

Pair after pair skated and Jansen remained in first place until only Scott, the former world record holder, had a chance to defeat him.

As Scott came down the stretch for the last 100 meters, the crowd roared again. But the cheers were not for Scott. Rather, the thousands in the stands knew that Dan Jansen had finally won the gold medal.

"Even the guys I was skating against that day said 'I hope you win today,'" Jansen recalled. "When they announced my time in the locker room, the skaters were cheering. That, to me, was just as rewarding—that my competition felt that way about me."

Later, Jansen stood on the top step of the awards podium as the national anthem played in his honor.

"I didn't know if I was going to break down and just be crying up there," he recalled with a smile. "All I could think of was my family: my wife, Robin. My daughter, Jane. But mostly I thought of my sister Jane because the Dan Jansen story began with her death. And now it could finally end."

As the strains of the national anthem came to a close, Jansen raised his eyes skyward and saluted.

"I knew this would be the last time that I could tell the world about my sister Jane. She was so special and so courageous. And I thought it only right that I salute her."

After the awards ceremony, the lights of the arena darkened and a spotlight shone on Jansen as he took the victory lap reserved for Olympic champions. Slowly, he skated around the track to the cheering of the thousands. Then he moved toward the stands and paused for a moment. His 9-month-old daughter, Jane, was handed to him, and he continued his victory lap, his arms cradling his daughter.

A few minutes before, Dan Jansen had paid tribute to his sister. Now those moments were shared with the daughter who bears her name. And perhaps that is the way it should be, for it has been written that "with every ending, there is a new beginning."

WINTER OLYMPIC SITES

	Year	Site	Nations	Total	Men	Women
Winter Events*	1908	London, England	5	21	14	7
Winter Events*	1920	Antwerp, Belgium	10	86	74	12
1st Winter Games	1924	Chamonix, France	16	258	245	13
2nd Winter Games	1928	St. Moritz, Switzerland	25	464	438	26
3rd Winter Games	1932	Lake Placid, New York	17	252	231	21
4th Winter Games	1936	Garmisch-Partenkirchen, Germany	28	668	588	80
5th Winter Games	1948	St. Moritz, Switzerland	28	669	592	77
6th Winter Games	1952	Oslo, Norway	30	694	585	109
7th Winter Games	1956	Cortina d'Ampezzo, Italy	32	820	688	132
8th Winter Games	1960	Squaw Valley, California	30	665	522	143
9th Winter Games	1964	Innsbruck, Austria	36	1,091	891	200
10th Winter Games	1968	Grenoble, France	37	1,158	947	211
11th Winter Games	1972	Sapporo, Japan	35	1,006	800	206
12th Winter Games	1976	Innsbruck, Austria	37	1,123	892	231
13th Winter Games	1980	Lake Placid, New York	37	1,072	839	233
14th Winter Games	1984	Sarajevo, Yugoslavia	49	1,274	1,000	274
15th Winter Games	1988	Calgary, Canada	57	1,423	1,110	313
16th Winter Games	1992	Albertville, France	64	1,801	1,313	488
17th Winter Games	1994	Lillehammer, Norway	67	1,844	1,302	542
18th Winter Games	1998	Nagano, Japan				
19th Winter Games	2002	Salt Lake City, Utah				

*Although figure skating was an event at both the 1908 and 1920 Games, and an ice hockey tournament was contested in 1920, an authorized, official Olympic Winter Games did not emerge until 1924.

RECORDS OF THE
WINTER OLYMPIC GAMES
PROVIDED COURTESY OF BILL MALLON

Most Medals

10	Raisa Smetanina (URS/EUN-NSK)
9	Sixten Jernberg (SWE-NSK)
9	Lyubov Egorova (EUN/RUS-NSK)
8	Bjørn Dæhlie (NOR-NSK)
8	Karin Kania-Enke (GDR-SSK)
8	Galina Kulakova (URS-NSK)
7	Seven athletes tied with seven.

Most Gold Medals

6	Lydia Skoblikova (URS-SSK)
6	Lyubov Egorova (EUN/RUS-NSK)
5	Bonnie Blair (USA-SSK)
5	Bjørn Dæhlie (NOR-NSK)
5	Eric Heiden (USA-SSK)
5	Clas Thunberg (FIN-SSK)
4	Eleven athletes tied with four.

Most Silver Medals

5	Andrea Ehrig-Schöne-Mitscherlich (GDR-SSK)
5	Raisa Smetanina (URS/EUN-NSK)
5	Bogdan Musiol (GDR/GER-BOB)
4	Karin Kania-Enke (GDR-SSK)
4	Hilkka Riihivuori-Kuntola (FIN-NSK)
4	Vladimir Smirnov (URS/EUN/KAZ-NSK)

Most Bronze Medals

5	Harri Kirvesniemi (FIN-NSK)

4	Marja-Liisa Kirvesniemi-Hämäläinen (FIN-NSK)
4	Roald Larsen (NOR-SSK)
4	Elena Välbe (EUN-NSK)
3	Nine athletes tied with three.

Most Years Between Appearances

20	John Heaton (USA-LUG/SKE; 1928–48)
20	Max Houben (BEL BOB; 1928–48)
20	Riccardo "Bibi" Torriani (SUI-ICH; 1928–48)
20	Stanislaw Marusarz (POL-NSK; 1932–52)
20	Frank Stack (CAN-SSK; 1932–52)
20	James Bickford (USA-BOB; 1936–56)
20	Sepp Bradl (AUT-NSK; 1936–56)
20	Carl-Erik Eriksson (SWE-BOB; 1964–84)
20	Colin Coates (AUS-SSK; 1968–88)

Most Medals, Women

10	Raisa Smetanina (URS/EUN-NSK)
9	Lyubov Egorova (EUN/RUS-NSK)
8	Karin Kania-Enke (GDR-SSK)
8	Galina Kulakova (URS-NSK)
7	Andrea Ehrig-Schöne-Mitscherlich (GDR-SSK)
7	Marja-Liisa Kirvesniemi-Hämäläinen (FIN-NSK)
6	Lydia Skoblikova (URS-SSK)
6	Bonnie Blair (USA-SSK)

Most Gold Medals, Women

6	Lydia Skoblikova (URS-SSK)
6	Lyubov Egorova (EUN/RUS-NSK)
5	Bonnie Blair (USA-SSK)

4	Galina Kulakova (URS-NSK)
4	Raisa Smetanina (URS/EUN-NSK)
3	Eight athletes tied with three.

Most Silver Medals, Women

5	Andrea Ehrig-Schöne-Mitscherlich (GDR-SSK)
5	Raisa Smetanina (URS/EUN-NSK)
4	Karin Kania-Enke (GDR-SSK)
4	Hilkka Riihivuori-Kuntola (FIN-NSK)
3	Eight athletes tied with three.

Most Bronze Medals, Women

4	Marja-Liisa Kirvesniemi-Hämäläinen (FIN-NSK)
4	Yelena Välbe (EUN-NSK)
3	Stefania Belmondo (ITA-NSK)
3	Alevtina Kolchina (URS-NSK)
3	Marjo Matikainen (FIN-NSK)
3	Natalya Petruseva (URS-SSK)
3	Gabriele Zange-Schönbrunn (GDR-SSK)

Most Years Winning Medals, Women

5	Raisa Smetanina (URS/EUN-NSK)
4	Galina Kulakova (URS-NSK)
3	Seventeen athletes tied with three.

Most Years Winning Gold Medals, Women

3	Bonnie Blair (USA-SSK)
3	Sonja Henie (NOR-FSK)
3	Anfisa Reztsova (URS/EUN/RUS-BIA-NSK)
3	Irina Rodnina (URS-FSK)
3	Raisa Smetanina (URS/EUN-NSK)
2	Nineteen athletes tied with two.

Most Years Between Medals, Women

16	Raisa Smetanina (URS/EUN-NSK)
12	Andrea Ehrig-Schöne-Mitscherlich (GDR-SSK)
12	Phyllis Johnson (GBR-FSK)
12	Alevtina Kolchina (URS-NSK)
12	Galina Kulakova (URS-NSK)

Most Years Between Gold Medals, Women

16	Raisa Smetanina (URS/EUN-NSK)
8	Sonja Henie (NOR-FSK)
8	Marie-Thêrès Nadig (SUI-ASK)
8	Irina Rodnina (URS-FSK)
6	Five athletes tied with six.

Most Appearances, Women

6	Marja-Liisa Kirvesniemi-Hämäläinen (FIN-NSK; 1976–94)
5	Monika Gawenus-Holzner-Pflug (FRG-SSK;1972–88)
5	Raisa Smetanina (URS/EUN-NSK;1976–92)

Most Years Between Appearances, Women

18	Marja-Liisa Kirvesniemi-Hämäläinen (FIN-NSK; 1976–94)
16	Monika Gawenus-Holzner-Pflug (FRG-SSK;1972–88)
16	Raisa Smetanina (URS/EUN-NSK; 1976–92)
12	Fifteen athletes tied with twelve.

Most Medals, Men

9	Sixten Jernberg (SWE-NSK)
8	Bjørn Dæhlie (NOR-NSK)
7	Ivar Ballangrud (NOR-SSK)
7	Veikko Hakulinen (FIN-NSK)
7	Eero Mäantyranta (FIN-NSK)
7	Bogdan Musiol (GDR/GER-BOB)
7	Clas Thunberg (FIN-SSK)

Most Gold Medals, Men

5	Bjørn Dæhlie (NOR-NSK)
5	Eric Heiden (USA-SSK)
5	Clas Thunberg (FIN-SSK)
4	Nine athletes tied with four.

Most Silver Medals, Men

5	Bogdan Musiol (GDR/GER-BOB)
4	Vladimir Smirnov (URS/EUN/KAZ-NSK)
3	Eleven athletes tied with three.

Most Bronze Medals, Men

5	Harri Kirvesniemi (FIN-NSK)
4	Roald Larsen (NOR-SSK)
3	Hans van Helden (NED-SSK)
3	Pavel Kolchin (URS-NSK)
3	Klaus Sulzenbacher (AUT-NSK)
3	Leo Visser (NED-SSK)

Most Years Winning Medals, Men

4	Gillis Grafström (SWE-FSK)
4	Jiří Holík (CZE-ICH)
4	Wolfgang Hoppe (GDR/GER-BOB)
4	Harri Kirvesniemi (FIN-NSK)
4	Bogdan Musiol (GDR/GER-BOB)
4	Alexander Tikhonov (URS-BIA)
4	Vladislav Tretiak (URS-ICH)

Most Years Winning Two or More Medals, Men

3	Sixten Jernberg (SWE-NSK; 1956, 1960, 1964)
3	Eugenio Monti (ITA-BOB; 1956, 1964, 1968)
3	Bogdan Musiol (GDR-BOB; 1980, 1984, 1988)
2	Thirty-six athletes tied with two.

Most Years Winning Gold Medals, Men

4	Alexander Tikhonov (URS-BIA)
3	Eleven athletes tied with three.

Most Years Between Medals, Men

20	John Heaton (USA-LUG/SKE)
20	Riccardo "Bibi" Torriani (SUI-ICH)
16	Fritz Feierabend (SUI-BOB)
16	Birger Ruud (NOR-NSK)
14	Harri Kirvesniemi (FIN-NSK)
14	Tomas Jonsson (SWE-ICH)
14	Mats Naslund (SWE-ICH)
12	Eleven athletes tied with twelve.

Most Years Between Gold Medals, Men

12	Paul Hildgartner (ITA-LUG)
12	Alexander Tikhonov (URS-BIA)
12	Vladislav Tretiak (URS-ICH)
10	Jens Weißflog (GDR/GER-NSK)
8	Eleven athletes tied with eight.

Most Appearances, Men

6	Colin Coates (AUS-SSK; 1968–88)
6	Carl-Erik Eriksson (SWE-BOB; 1968–84)
6	Alfred Eder (AUT-BIA; 1976–92)
5	Oddvar Brå ((NOR-NSK; 1972–88)
5	Paul Hildgartner (ITA-LUG; 1972–88)
5	Örjan Sandler (SWE-SSK; 1964–80)
5	Udo Kießling (FRG/GER-ICH; 1976–92)
5	Jochen Behle (FRG/GER-NSK; 1980–94)
5	Sergey Danilin (URS/EUN/RUS; 1980–94)
5	Harri Kirvesniemi (FIN-NSK; 1980–94)
5	Bogdan Musiol (GDR/GER-BOB; 1980–94)

5	Hansjörg Raffl (ITA-BOB; 1980–94)
5	Petter Thoresen (NOR-ICH; 1980–94)

Most Years Between Appearances, Men

20	John Heaton (USA-LUG/SKE; 1928–48)
20	Max Houben (BEL-BOB; 1928–48)
20	Riccardo "Bibi" Torriani (SUI-ICH; 1928–48)
20	Stanislaw Marusarz (POL-NSK; 1932–52)
20	Frank Stack (CAN-SSK; 1932–52)
20	James Bickford (USA-BOB; 1936–56)
20	Sepp Bradl (AUT-NSK; 1936–56)
20	Carl-Erik Eriksson (SWE-BOB; 1964–84)
20	Colin Coates (AUT-SSK; 1968–88)

Youngest-Known Competitors

Yrs-Days

11-074	Cecilia Colledge (GBR-FSK, 1932)
11-108	Megan Taylor (GBR-FSK, 1932)
11-162	Beatrice Hustiu (ROM-FSK, 1968)
11-256	Liu Lu-Yang (CHN-FSK, 1988)
11-295	Sonja Henie (NOR-FSK, 1924)

Youngest Medalists

Yrs-Days

13-083	Kim Yoon-Mi (KOR-STK, 1994)
14-132	Won Hye-Kyung (KOR-STK, 1994)
14-363	Scott Ethan Allen (USA-FSK, 1964)
15-007	Manuela Groß (GDR-FSK, 1972)
15-068	Andrea Mitscherlich (GDR-SSK, 1976)
15-078	Cecilia Colledge (GBR-FSK, 1936)
15-091	Marina Cherkasova (URS-FSK, 1980)
15-127	Maxi Herber (GER-FSK, 1936)
15-129	Thomas Doe (USA-BOB, 1928)

| 15-260 | Ingrid Wendl (AUT-FSK; 1956) |

Oldest-Known Competitors

Yrs-Days

53-297	James Coats (GBR-SKE/LUG, 1948)
53-274	Carl-Erik Eriksson (SWE-BOB, 1984)
53-214	Matthias Stinnes (ARG-LUG, 1964)
52-300	John Amabile (PUR-BOB, 1992)
52-198	Harvey Hook (ISV-BOB, 1988)
52-144	Joseph Savage (USA-FSK, 1932)

Oldest Medalists

Yrs-Days

49-278	Max Houben (BEL-BOB, 1948)
48-357	Jay O'Brien (USA-BOB, 1932)
46-342	Albert Madörin (SUI-BOB, 1952)
46-298	Franz Kapus (SUI-BOB, 1956)
45-225	Edgar Syers (GBR-FSK, 1908)
45-040	Clifford Grey (USA-BOB, 1932)
44-361	Jay O'Brien (USA-BOB, 1928)
44-184	Geoffrey Hall-Say (GBR-FSK, 1908)
44-077	Martin Stixrud (NOR-FSK, 1920)
43-237	Fritz Feierabend (SUI-BOB, 1952)

MEDALS WON BY COUNTRIES

In the following tables, places are given according to total medals. The lists include the medals won in 1908 and 1920 figure skating (7 events) and 1920 ice hockey (1 event), which were actually contested as part of the Summer Olympics.

		G	S	B	Total
1.	Norway	73	77	64	214
2.	Soviet Union (1956–1988)	78	57	59	194
3.	United States	53	56	37	146
4.	Austria	36	48	44	128
5.	Finland	36	45	42	123
6.	German Democratic Republic (1956–1988)*	43	39	36	118
7.	Sweden	39	26	34	99
8.	Switzerland	27	29	29	85
9.	Italy	25	21	21	67
10.	Canada	19	20	25	64
11.	Germany (1908, 1928–1936, 1992–)*	23	21	17	61
12.	Federal Republic of Germany (1952–1988)*	18	20	19	57
13.	France	16	16	21	53
14.	The Netherlands	14	19	17	50
15.	Czechoslovakia	2	8	16	26
16.	Russia (1908, 1994–)	12	8	4	24
17.	Unified Team (1992)	9	6	8	23
18.	Great Britian	7	4	12	23
19.	Japan	3	8	8	19
20.	Korea (South)	6	2	2	10
21.	Liechtenstein	2	2	5	9
22.	China	—	4	2	6
23.	Hungary	—	2	4	6

*Between 1956 and 1964, athletes from East and West Germany competed as a combined team, though medal statistics were kept separate.

24.	Belgium	1	1	2	4
	Poland	1	1	2	4
26.	Yugoslavia	—	3	1	4
27.	Kazakhstan	1	2	—	3
28.	Slovenia	—	—	3	3
29.	Spain	1	—	1	2
	Ukraine	1	—	1	2
31.	Belarus	—	2	—	2
	Luxembourg	—	2	—	2
33.	DPR Korea (North)	—	1	1	2
34.	Uzbekistan	1	—	—	1
35.	New Zealand	—	1	—	1
36.	Australia	—	—	1	1
	Bulgaria	—	—	1	1
	Romania	—	—	1	1
Totals		547	551	540	1,638

COUNTRY ABBREVIATIONS
USED IN RECORDS
(SOME DIFFER FROM THE OFFICIAL IOC ABBREVIATIONS)

Argentina	ARG
Australia	AUS
Austria	AUT
Belarus	BLR
Belgium	BEL
Bulgaria	BUL
Canada	CAN
China	CHN
Czechoslovakia/Czech Republic	CZE
Democratic People's Republic of Korea (North)	PRK
Federal Republic of Germany (West)	FRG
Finland	FIN
France	FRA
German Democratic Republic (East)	GDR
Germany	GER
Great Britain	GBR
Hungary	HUN
Italy	ITA
Japan	JPN
Kazakhstan	KAZ
Korea (South)	KOR
Liechtenstein	LIE
Luxembourg	LUX
Netherlands	NED
New Zealand	NZL
Norway	NOR
Poland	POL
Puerto Rico	PUR
Romania	ROM
Russia	RUS
Slovakia	SVK
Slovenia	SLO
Soviet Union	URS
Spain	ESP
Sweden	SWE
Switzerland	SUI
Ukraine	UKR
Unified Team	EUN
United States	USA
Uzbekistan	UZB
Virgin Islands	ISV
Yugoslavia	YUG

SPORT ABBREVIATIONS
USED IN RECORDS

Alpine Skiing	ASK
Biathlon	BIA
Bobsled	BOB
Figure Skating	FSK
Ice Hockey	ICH
Luge	LUG
Nordic Skiing (Cross-Country, Jumping)	NSK
Skeleton (Sled)	SKE
Speed Skating	SSK
Speed Skating–Short Track	STK

PHOTO CREDITS

13	Allsport UK/Bob Martin
15	Courtesy of Cappy Productions, Inc.
18	Allsport UK
22	© USOC
24	UPI/Corbis-Bettmann
28	Courtesy of Bill Mallon
32	UPI/Corbis-Bettmann
34	UPI/Corbis-Bettmann
38	Allsport UK/Mike Powell
40	U.S. National Ski Hall of Fame
44	Courtesy of Colin Coates, photo by Leo Vogelenzang
46	Courtesy of Colin Coates
48	Courtesy of Bill Mallon
49	UPI/Corbis-Bettmann
50	UPI/Corbis-Bettmann
54	UPI/Corbis-Bettmann
56	Courtesy of Bill Mallon
60	© USOC
62	© USOC
66	Courtesy of Cappy Productions, Inc.
68	UPI/Corbis-Bettmann
72	Courtesy of Cappy Productions, Inc.
76	Courtesy of Cappy Productions, Inc.
80	Allsport UK/Pascal Rondeau
82	Allsport USA/Tony Duffy
84	Allsport USA/Mike Powell
86	Allsport UK
90	UPI/Corbis-Bettmann
91	UPI/Corbis-Bettmann
92	Allsport USA/Tony Duffy
96	UPI/Corbis-Bettmann
98	© Agence Vandystadt/Allsport, photo by Gerard Vandystadt
102	UPI/Corbis-Bettmann
103	Courtesy of Bill Mallon
104	© USOC
108	Long Photography
110	© Agence Vandystadt/Allsport, photo by Richard Martin
113	Allsport UK/Clive Brunskill
114	Courtesy of the U.S. Bobsled & Skeleton Federation
118	Underwood & Underwood/Corbis-Bettmann
120	UPI/Corbis-Bettmann
124	Courtesy of the Amateur Athletic Foundation
126	Allsport UK/Richard Martin
130	Courtesy of Cappy Productions, Inc.
132	Courtesy of Hayes and David Jenkins
136	© USOC
138	Allsport UK/Tony Duffy
142	Allsport UK/Pascal Rondeau
146	Courtesy of the Amateur Athletic Foundation
148	Allsport UK/Shaun Botterill
152	Allsport USA/(USOC)
154	Allsport UK/Steve Powell
158	© Agence Vandystadt/Allsport, photo by Richard Martin
160	Courtesy of Cappy Productions, Inc.
164	UPI/Corbis-Bettmann
166	UPI/Corbis-Bettmann
168	© USOC
170	Allsport UK/Clive Brunskill
172	Allsport UK/Steve Powell
176	© USOC
178	Courtesy of Cappy Productions, Inc.
182	Courtesy of Cappy Productions, Inc.
183	Courtesy of Cappy Productions, Inc.
184	© USOC
188	© Agence Vandystadt/Allsport, photo by Gerard Vandystadt
190	Allsport USA/Chris Cole